I0132051

Ray. S. Lineham

The Street Of Human Habitations

Ray. S. Lineham

The Street Of Human Habitations

ISBN/EAN: 9783742834454

Manufactured in Europe, USA, Canada, Australia, Japa

Cover: Foto ©Thomas Meinert / pixelio.de

Manufactured and distributed by brebook publishing software
(www.brebook.com)

Ray. S. Lineham

The Street Of Human Habitations

THE STREET OF HUMAN
HABITATIONS

RAMA VARMA RESEARCH INSTITUTE,
TRICHUR, COCHIN STATE.

THE STREET OF HUMAN HABITATIONS

BY

RAY S. LINEHAM

Member of the Japan Society

WITH NEARLY FOUR HUNDRED ILLUSTRATIONS

LONDON

CHAPMAN & HALL, Ltd.

1894

[*All rights reserved*]

DEDICATION

⸻

TO MY HUSBAND—AND CRITIC;

THESE CHAPTERS—WHOSE DEVELOPMENT HE WATCHED

AND ENCOURAGED WITH UNFLAGGING INTEREST

AND AN EVER READY PENCIL—ARE

AFFECTIONATELY INSCRIBED

PREFACE.

So much has already been written concerning the people you are about to visit with me, that it may be thought there is nothing left to write. True, many valuable and exhaustive books have been contributed to this section of our libraries—else had these pages never been penned; but is it not also true that, just in proportion as they are valuable and exhaustive, these works are costly and inaccessible, and that therefore the most of us know little or nothing at all about them? The world to-day is too busy with vital questions of food, raiment, and the gold that perisheth, to care much about how the world of yesterday lived and moved and had its being; or if it does care, has, in its ever-increasing fight for existence and its ever-narrowing leisure for literature, no time for the research which monumental works demand. It needs its mental food not only selected, but peptonized—partially digested—by proxy, and dished up ready for absorption. If, then, in my choice of dainties from dusty shelves that are not

always easy of access ; in my semi-digestion of them,
and more especially in my particular manner of dishing
them up, I succeed in providing a toothsome repast ;
if I, above all, whet your appetite for the fare provided
by *chefs* far greater than I, then am I well content.

The first three chapters of this volume were already
in my publisher's hands when M. Maspero's charming
account of the ancient Egyptians and Assyrians
appeared—perhaps the most popular book on the subject that has ever been written. My Egyptian and
Assyrian chapters were originally written for and
produced in *Science and Art*, but the space available
for illustrations was small, and on revising them for
publication in book form, I accepted most gratefully
the offer of such illustrations as I might select from
M. Maspero's work. I make this statement because of
a certain similarity in the conception of M. Maspero's
work and mine, and it is due to the former to say that,
dealing with two instead of nine races of men, the
author has given much delightful detail which is not
included in this book ; while to myself is due the
statement that the latter was entirely mapped out in
ignorance of the other work in progress at the same
time.

In addition to the illustrations already referred to, I
am indebted to my publishers for a very large number
of others—chiefly from the works of MM. Perrot and
Chipiez on "Ancient Egyptian, Chaldean, Phœnician,
and Persian Art"; to the Department of Science and

Art at South Kensington for the use of drawings in its excellent series of "Handbooks"; to Mr. Duncan C. Dallas for courteous permission to copy a print of his fine "Dallastype" of the Deluge Tablet in the British Museum; to Professor W. Flinders-Petrie, who generously placed the whole of his recent Tel-el-Amarna "finds" at my disposal; and to my friend Frances Crawford for much valuable assistance in preparing various drawings for the press.

I desire also to acknowledge the ready help of many friends in the preparation of the letterpress. More especially would I thank my fellow-members of the Japan Society—Mr. Daigoro Goh, Chancellor of the Imperial Consulate of Japan, who has done me the honour of revising the proof sheets of my chapter on Japan; Mr. A. Diósy, founder and Co-Hon. Sec. (with Mr. Goh) of the Japan Society, whose wide knowledge of the customs of all lands has been of the utmost service to me; and Mr. John Mogford, Librarian and Curator of the same excellent Institution, whose wise and learned counsel and kindly sympathy have been untiring throughout the whole of my work.

Finally, the lectures, and the "Transactions and Proceedings" of that much needed and widely appreciated Anglo-Oriental Institution already mentioned—the Japan Society—have enlightened me on many important and obscure points connected with the wonderful "Islands of the Dragon-fly."

"Our Street" has for me a never-failing interest and

fascination, and I am sorry that, for the present, we can only explore one side of it. Greek and Roman, Norseman and Celt, Aztec and African all invite us; perhaps some day we shall also visit *them* together.

RAY S. LINEHAM.

JESMOND, LEE, KENT.
January, 1894.

CONTENTS.

CHAPTER I.

MEN OF BONE AND MEN OF STONE.

CHAPTER II.

MEN OF METAL.

CHAPTER III.

AN AGE OF IRON.

CHAPTER IV.

THE LAND OF THE LOTUS.

CHAPTER V.

"BY THE WATERS OF BABYLON."

CHAPTER VI.

A REGION OF PALM.

CHAPTER VII.

PLAINS OF WILD ALMOND.

CHAPTER VIII.

THE ISLAND OF THE ROSE-APPLE.

CHAPTER IX.

THE CHILDREN OF FUJI SAN.

PRINCIPAL BOOKS
CONSULTED FOR THIS WORK.

PREHISTORIC.

Sir John Lubbock's " Prehistoric Times."
 " " "Condition of Primitive Men."
Sir John Evans' " Ancient Stone Implements."
Canon Greenwell's " British Barrows."
Boyd-Dawkins' " Cave Hunting."
Quatrefage's " Human Species."
Nadaillac's "Prehistoric Peoples."
Joly's "Man before Metals."
E. B. Taylor's "Researches into the Early History of Mankind."
Day's " Prehistoric Use of Iron and Steel."
Hunter-Duvar's " Stone, Bronze, and Iron Ages."
Worsae's " Danish Art."

EGYPT.

Sir J. Wilkinson's " Popular Account of the Ancient Egyptians."
Marquis Spineto's " Egyptian Antiquities and Hieroglyphics."
Professor Petrie's " Ten Years' Digging."
 " " " Medum."
Palmer's " Egyptian Chronicles."
Lenormant's " Beginnings of History."
Perrot and Chipiez's " History of Art in Ancient Egypt."
Marriette Bey's " Monuments of Upper Egypt."
Vyse's " Pyramids of Gizeh."
Ferguson's " Handbook of Architecture."

ASSYRIA AND CHALDEA.

Canon Rawlinson's "Religions of the Ancient World."
  „   „   "Seven Great Monarchies."
Professor Sayce's "Assyria."
  „   „   "Early Chaldean Empire."
  „   „   "History of Sennacherib."
Lenormant's "Chaldean Magic."
Sir Henry Layard's "Art of the Ancient Assyrians."
  „   „   "Nineveh and Babylon."
George Smith's "Assyria."
  „   „   "Chaldean Account of Genesis."
Budge's "History of Esarhaddon."
  „   "Babylonian Life and History."

PHŒNICIA.

Perrot and Chipiez's "History of Ancient Art in Phœnicia
    and her Dependencies."
Perrot and Chipiez's "History of Ancient Art in Phrygia,
    Caria, Lycia."
Professor Church's "Carthage."
Myer's "Lost Empires."
Duncker's "History of Antiquity."
Sayce's "Ancient Empires of the East."

PERSIA.

Perrot and Chipiez's "Ancient Art in Persia."
R. M. Smith's "Persian Art."
Oliver's "Across the Border."
Clousen's "Arabian Poetry."
  „   "Some Persian Tales."
Loftus's "Travels and Researches."
De Windt's "Ride across Persia."

INDIA.

Rhys David's "Buddhism."
Max Müller's "Sacred Hymns of the Brahmins."
Acland's "Manners and Customs of India."
Sir W. W. Hunter's "History of India."
Sir George Birdwood's "Industrial Arts of India."
Sir Edwin Arnold's "Indian Idylls."
Day's "Folk Tales of Bengal."

JAPAN.

Chamberlain's "Things Japanese."
Satow's "Handbook for Japan."
Miss Bird's "Unbeaten Tracks."
Frank's "Japanese Pottery."
Von. Siebold's "Manners and Customs of the Japanese."
Purcell's "A Suburb of Yedo."
Griffis' "Japan, in History, Folk Lore, and Art."
Rein's "Japan."
Batchelor's "The Ainu of Japan."
Morse's "Japanese Homes."
Sir Ed. Reed's "Japan."
The first volume of "Transactions and Proceedings of the
Japan Society."

RAMA VARMA RESEARCH INSTITUTE.
TRICHUR, COCHIN STATE.

THE

STREET OF HUMAN HABITATIONS.

CHAPTER I.

MEN OF BONE AND MEN OF STONE.

It is a long street, and a steep street, and I am afraid
that in some parts it is also a very dark street. Not
particularly interesting at first sight, perhaps, and you
could suggest others much more worthy of considera-
tion, you think; but wait. I may tell you at the
outset that my street is not a common street, and, in
interest, far exceeds the grandest you can point out to
me. It has its rows of dwellings like other streets, it
is true, but these have taken, not one, but countless
ages to build, and the skill of as many architects has
been lavished upon them. It is the street you know
most about, and yet least, for it is the street you live
in, that your fathers lived in before you, and in which
your children must live after you. Has it then no
interest? Have you never wondered what kind of
people are to be found in this street, which has been
your home so long that it has, from mere familiarity,
become just a little stale and commonplace to you? If
you have not already made their acquaintance, I think
you will be surprised to find how much there is that
you would like to know about the good folk who live a
great many doors further down.

I have said that my street is long and steep, so we must begin our journey betimes, in the misty light that comes betwixt darkness and dawn, and when the form of man at least is still dim as he emerges from an eternity of night. But before you venture on this voyage of discovery, would you not like a bird's-eye view of the ground over which we propose to travel? Very good. Only I must ask you to take two steps—one over space, the other, a backward step this, over time—and we will now, if you please, enter the Paris Exhibition by the Pont de Jéna in, say July, 1889.

As you stand with me on the second storey of the Eiffel Tower (the view is clearer there than from the summit) and behold the glorious panorama stretched out at your feet; as the far-off boundaries of the Exhibition gradually unfold before you, and you count the bridges of wood, of iron, and of stone, which, whether they span the silver thread of the Seine, or a street seething with traffic, all bind the main trunk and its many limbs into one living whole; as you grasp some idea of the immense area in which is laid out the most varied, the most stupendous, the most perfect display of the work of man's hands, and of his teeming brain, that has ever been gathered together in any age, it is not surprising that you are bewildered and even beg me to abandon our projected journey, for, not having any good reason to suppose that your span of life will be a longer one than your neighbours', you begin to think twice before setting out to investigate a domain so vast.

Do not be in such a hurry, my friend. I will not occupy either your time or my own in traversing the Paris Exhibition. We are only here, you must remember, that you may be shown one picture, the details of which we shall examine more closely together later. I have never had much respect myself for books without pictures, or for songs without words; they call for a

fund of imagination I do not pretend to possess, and
would rather not exercise if I did. After listening to
ninety-nine renderings, more or less abstruse, of one
and the same theme, I have decided that the game is
not worth the candle, and that I prefer an easier
method of conveying information. Most people can
understand a picture when they see it, and in my
humble opinion it would be just as well if the artist's
brush had a little more to do, and the author's pen a
little less, in those fountains of good and evil—our
schools and colleges.

Here, then, under the shadow of that colossal
modern Pharos, whose fiery eye laughs at the darkness
of night, and lays her secrets bare for many a mile
around, you will find a lecture-theatre unique in the
world's history, where the lessons are taught plainly
enough for those who care to read them. Everything
speaks of a country successful beyond the seas, and
contented and prosperous at home, and you begin to
wonder whether this can be the same people who, just
a century ago bathed themselves in blood—the finest,
the bravest, the most sacred in all France—the blood
of king, warrior, and priest; the blood of men, women,
and little children—blood which poured like a river
down those streets so clean and fair to-day.

After surfeit comes sorrow. An expiatory altar must
be raised, and the ghosts of the martyrs laid; the
amour propre of the murderers is re-established, and
the haunting cry of the slain forgotten. Oh, fickle
people! to-day the vast multitude on the Field of
Mars is gathered to commemorate those scenes of terror
and bloodshed, and every voice is eager to proclaim
the benefits the nation owes to the work of butcher
and regicide. A chequered record, indeed, that of
France; and the last pages still unwritten!

And the picture? yes, of course; I had not forgotten
—here it is. You are a little disappointed? Only a

long row of buildings of divers forms and of natural size
extending to a distance of about two hundred yards on
either hand of the bridge we crossed a few minutes
ago. Ah! it is a book of instruction, this street of
human habitations! Turk and Troglodyte, Aztec and
Assyrian, Jew and Jap—ay, the peoples of the earth
are here, all eager to teach, as ever you to learn. But
the hours are passing—passing; and we have many a

Cave Dwelling.   Hut of Irish Elk Age.

mile to go before our day's work is done, many an age
to retrace, thousands of years before Noah preached
the story of the Flood; so let us descend and begin.

In the street we are entering you see there on the
right a large empty space, and on the left a wide forest
of pine, between us and the first dwelling. These you
may consider, if you like, the abode of the very earliest
specimens of the *genus homo*. Not much shelter from

wind and wet here (on the right, at least), and it is to
be hoped that they - the aforesaid specimens—were
not treated to so many varied samples of weather as
we are favoured with now-a-days, or the prehistoric
medicine-man must have had his hands full. Now let
us pass on to No. 1. Our progenitors have evidently
agreed that something more elaborate must be looked
up if they are to keep a sound tooth in their heads, or
a bone in their body free from rheumatism. But even
in these early days the labour question appears to have
been well digested, for no man troubles himself to build
so long as he can appropriate a dwelling ready to his

The Great Cave Bear.

hand, and the happy idea strikes him that the shelter
of a cave or a boulder will be better than no shelter at
all ; so the cave bears and hyenas—who long ago came
to the same conclusion—are evicted, and the " superior"
animal establishes himself comfortably, and to his own
entire satisfaction, in the vacant apartments. Cosy
enough are those early cave-dwellings, impervious alike
to winter's snow and summer's sun ; not much to boast
of in the way of light perhaps, but in other respects
decidedly better than the skin-built extinguishers on
the other side of the street, under which the belles of
Irish elk celebrity hide their charms, and in which
the accommodation is, to say the least of it, somewhat
limited.

As you come before the habitations of a people so remote, have you not a wild desire to wield for once the
magician's wand, summon those silent ones from the
oblivion of ages, and place them again in the homes
where they lived and laboured, loved and hated, so long
ago? Stand aside with me for a moment. Look at the
mouth of that cavern. A shadowy group is slowly
gathering; now it is more distinct. There is a large
flat rock in the centre, and beside it, seated on smaller
fragments, there are two women, one much younger than
the other, and quite pretty in spite of her coppery skin,

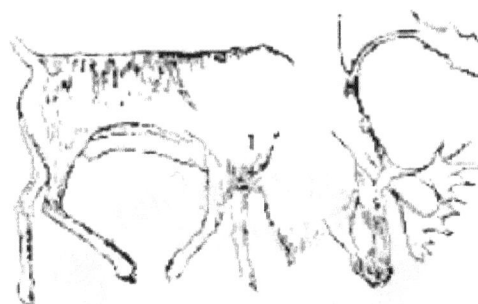

Carved Reindeer.

and you wonder, is she wife, or is the other? Clothing
they have none, unless you count the necklaces of
claws strung on thongs of skin, which are round their
necks, and the long masses of fine black hair, which
many a modern beauty would be proud of. They are
engaged in scratching something on pieces of bone, and
they use the flat rock as table and rough flints as tools.
Look closer, and you will find no mean skill displayed;
horses, fishes, deer, are all portrayed with a fidelity
that surprises you. I tell you, many a would-be
artist of to-day might, with profit, study the palæolithic
sketch-block. Your interest deepens as you notice the
implements of bone which lie about in every direction

—knives, fish-hooks, arrows, and needles so exquisitely
polished and pointed, and with eyes so accurately
drilled, that you may well admire the skill and
patience which, aided only by a sharp flint, can produce such results. Not content with etching on bone,
these primeval artists can show you actual sculpture.

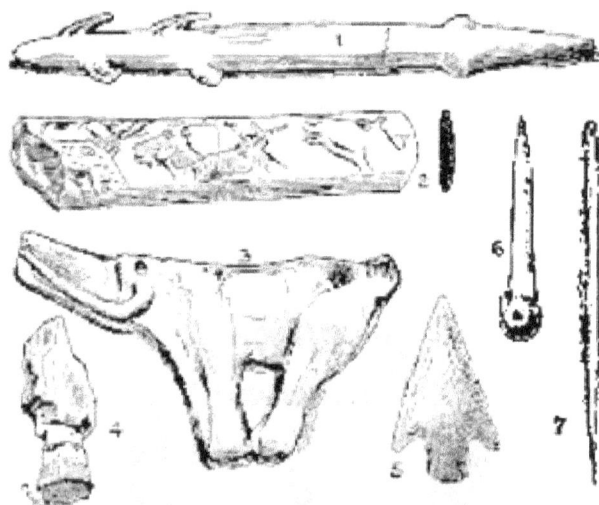

Palæolithic Bone Carving.—1. Bone harpoon. 2. Etching on
bone. 3. Sculpture in reindeer horn: a mammoth. 6. Bone
pin. 7. Bone needle.
Neolithic Flint Work.—4. Flint core, showing how the flakes
were struck off. 5. Flint arrow-head, finely finished by
chipping only. (From the British Museum; about half
natural size.)

Here, for example, is an excellent model of a mammoth,
carved out of a reindeer horn, and intended as handle
for a flint dagger, while elsewhere you may see objects
still more remarkable. The flints they use are but
roughly chipped, only sufficient pains being expended
to render them useful. All the resources of ornament

are reserved for articles of bone. They are, moreover,
by no means ignorant of colour, and I could show you
quantities of yellow ochre, red chalk and black lead,
stored away in little bone and shell receptacles ready
to be ground to powder in hollow pebbles. The pig-
ment is applied pretty profusely to their bodies on
state occasions, and is not altogether intended for
decoration, but is found—especially in summer—to
afford considerable protection from the bites and stings
of insects. There is no denying, however, that the
bone and stone folk, men as well as maidens, do indulge

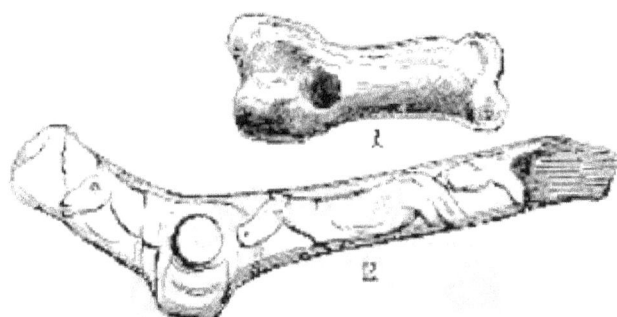

1. Prehistoric Whistle.   2. Wand of Office with a single hole.

in finery, for many varieties of amulets and ornaments
lie before you in this house of theirs. Clay beads,
fossils, fish bones, tusks, shells, teeth ; all pierced and
carved for use as adornments. One sturdy warrior
owns a unique necklace of forty bears' and three
lions' teeth, doubly precious of course as evidence of
his own prowess. The ladies, not being in a position
to acquire jewellery of this kind, collect bright stones
and shells, and form them into trinkets. Cockle-shells
are particularly favoured, but the prehistoric Scotch-
woman uses limpets and nerites. It is by no means
easy to understand the purpose of all the objects you
see around you. Here, for instance, is a beautifully

decorated bone which is certainly not intended as a tool. Those who ought to know say it is a kind of wand of office, and that the exact importance of the holder is represented by the number of holes perforating it.

In times fraught with so many dangers, it is often necessary to call in the help of a neighbour. And the bone carver has learnt to make a very decent whistle from the material at his disposal; he has gone further even, and out of two slender bird-bones has constructed a flute with which to while away the long dark evenings at his cheerless hearth. The sounds produced are unmistakably musical, if a little monotonous. These ancient people are of necessity hunters or fishers—sometimes both. They have not yet thought of making nets, and most of their fish are caught by harpooning, but they are a fearless race, and do not hesitate to encounter the perils of the sea in craft which you and I would not dare to enter. How the first boat came to be conceived is more than I can tell you; perhaps the torn-up trunk of a tree, flung during a storm into some river, and borne along on its rushing waters suggested it. Trimming up the ends and hollowing out would soon follow, but a long interval undoubtedly passed before a sail was dreamt of. Sails and nets are twin brothers, so it is natural that when the former make their appearance we find our palæolithic friends also using coarse nets, weighted by stones or broken pottery, and floated with pieces of bark.

Here comes a man, evidently from the chase; a brawny, fierce fellow, with whom the scarcely more fierce denizens of the woods must have had a hard time of it, if we may judge by the carcase on his back, and the long strings of claws, teeth, and bits of carved bone which encircle his waist, or are slung across from shoulder to hip. As he approaches, the women look up, and the younger smiles good-humouredly, but keeps her seat. The elder rises rather wearily, and to her is

thrown the reinforcement for the larder. Again you
wonder, which is wife to this man, or are both? Has
the dusky young beauty supplanted the help-meet of
the warrior's earlier days, or is it the mother, old and
ugly, who only lives a drudge in the savage ménage?

But there is a very noisy party in the adjacent
dwelling, and we may as well see what all the commotion is about. It is a cave very similar to that we
have just quitted, but this time we will make ourselves
more at home, if you don't mind; so step inside. A
dark passage leads to a still darker apartment, and but
for the distant babel of voices we should be puzzled
to know which of its many diverging alleys to take: as
it is, we are pretty safe in following that to the right.
It soon brings us to a short flight of natural rock steps,
on descending which we suddenly find ourselves en
famille. But they are in sad trouble, these people,
and too much engrossed with their own affairs to pay
any attention to you, so you need not be so apprehen-
sive. Besides, the place is so dark that you may stand
in this recess and watch them without any fear of
detection. There is a light indeed, but it flickers fit-
fully—what else could you expect from a wick of moss
stuck in the oily stomach of a dead penguin? In the
middle of the chamber a weeping mother clings to her
stricken boy, who writhes and foams in the paroxysms
of epilepsy. Several other inmates bemoan him with
loud cries. The father alone, stern and impassive,
listens silently while a third individual, evidently a
man who expects to be listened to, lays down the law
regarding the treatment of the case. The child is
beloved of the gods, but an evil spirit has possessed
him. A door must be opened, therefore, and the demon
ejected. The father remains silent. The speaker,
without more ado, takes the matter into his own hands.
Setting the poor boy, quite unconscious now, on a low
stone seat, he bids the parents support him, while he

himself proceeds to lay back a lock of the thick brown
hair on the side of the victim's head, and, first making
a T-shaped incision with a smooth flint, he scrapes
away a portion of the skin, and finally removes very
skilfully a disc of bone. The operation is over, and
you breathe freely again. Do not fear, small doubt
that the little one will recover; palæolithic trepanning

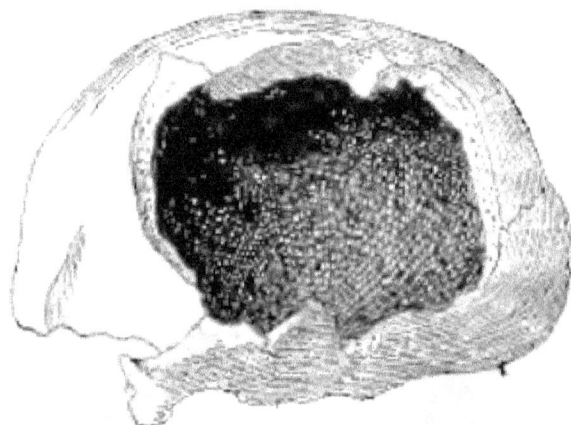

Trepanned Skull found in a Dolmen.

Disc of Bone from a trepanned skull.

very rarely has a fatal issue. As for the disc of bone,
that becomes the mother's most precious amulet. No
fear of fiend or goblin for her so long as that hangs
round her neck! And the boy; well, if he recover he
will be venerated through life; and after death many
more discs will be taken from his crown, each, however, having a tiny bit of the old cicatrix attached, as
a sort of hall mark, not to be dispensed with on any
account. Into his own dead, mutilated skull they will

probably put two or three such discs of more ancient date, so that, in the other world, he may not lose by the abstraction of so much of his anatomy. And as you picture to yourself the probable sequel of to-day's surgery, the figures recede, dimmer and dimmer now, and are lost.

It is a long stride from these rough-flint, bone-working Troglodytes, to the next people in our street of habitations. Perhaps no part of the street is so dark as that which divides the cave-men from their neolithic children. Trackless pine forests, resistless river torrents, vast mountains of fire, still vaster mountains of ice, upheavals, subsidences, deluge, annihilation! A terrible catalogue, which has taken thousands of years to write, yet all buried in that yawning chasm before you. And now the air grows chill; the snow falls thick and fast; every tree puts on a garment of purity, and not a footfall breaks the awful solitude. Faster and faster come the blinding flakes, until hill and valley join hands and are as one. Then breaks upon you the fierceness of an Arctic winter. The ice snaps and crackles at every step, and the keen air catches your every breath. Nearer and nearer creeps that icy sea, silently and pitilessly, until all animate things, nay the whole face of Nature, are lost in one common tomb.

But take heart of grace, my friend; we are safely over that wide gap, and whatever may have been the condition of the men we have passed on the way, one thing is certain, we are about to meet those who have made a decided advance towards civilization. No one can for a moment confound the beautiful weapons and tools of flint we now see with the rudely-chipped instruments of the cave-men. This later age is essentially one of *polished* stone, and we are again compelled to admire the patience and ingenuity of beings who, with such meagre resources at their disposal, can yet fashion weapons so remarkable.   Every

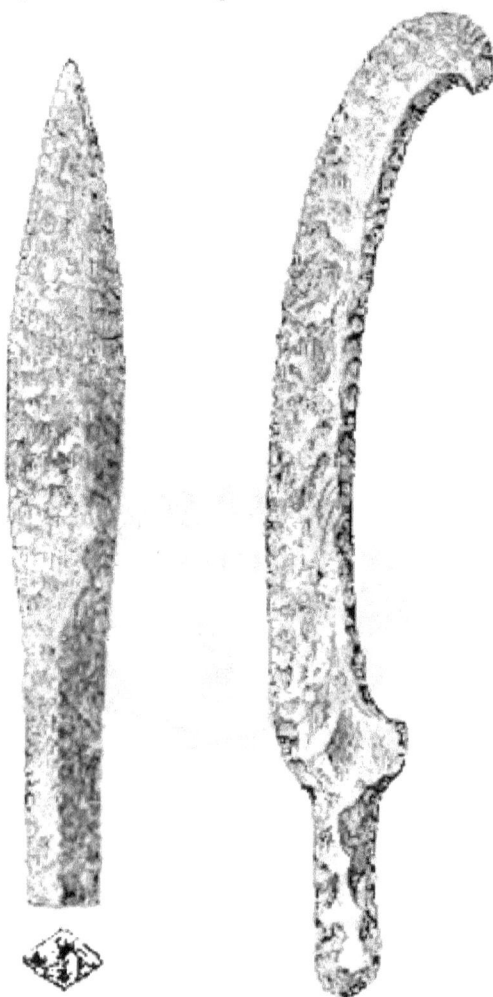

1. Stone Dagger.   2. Finely chipped Sickle.

kind of stone which is hard enough and tough enough

for the purpose is now employed for the manufacture
of implements; but flint is, without doubt, the one
most extensively used.   Its hardness and peculiar mode
of fracture recommend it before all others for the production of a good cutting instrument.   A well-directed
blow at any angle of a sound block of flint will detach
a flake, which, with a little grinding and polishing,
makes a very respectable knife.   But it is worth your
notice that, while a marked improvement is visible in
the finish of implements in this epoch, art, as applied
to the representation of animate objects, has declined.

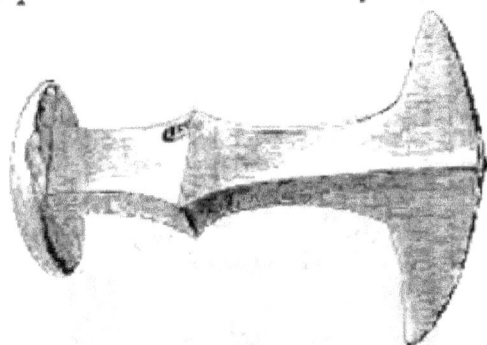

Stone Hammer.

No such spirited sketches occur here as those we saw
in the bone caves.   There is, however, a first attempt
at pottery, and the vessels, rude as they are, do not
lack decoration.   The potter's wheel is, of course, unknown, and the lines and patterns are produced in the
soft clay with sharp pointed stones, or even a finger
nail.   But you may examine the neolithic workshop for
yourself if you like.

Without, at one side of the door, a lad is preparing
salt, by burning a marine plant and pouring sea water
over the hot ashes.   Opposite is an old woman making
the family dinner, and a very excellent menu will be provided.   Into a rather tipsy-looking clay jar she puts a

fine blackcock and a lump of aurochs' flesh, plenty of water and some salt, and you have the soup, for it will stew nicely by means of those hot round pebbles she is dropping in. Now for the fish. In a hole scooped in the ground, between alternate layers of hot cinders, are placed eel, flounders, cod and herrings, oysters, mussels, and periwinkles, with over all a layer of fir-branches and an immense clod; and you may safely leave your second course to bake. A haunch of venison, an abundance of nuts, cherries, and plums, will complete a very appetizing repast, while the *débris* goes to swell that huge

Neolithic Pottery.

evil-smelling heap behind the house, the "kitchen midden," in fact!

Within, three people are busy at work. As in a previous picture, two are women—has this sort of thing existed *always*, I wonder? In the present case, however, a pretty equal division has been arrived at, and each is doing her own share. The clothing is still scanty, scarcely more than a strip of deer-skin, but there is now an expression of increased intelligence, which tells of a wider knowledge of men and things. They are sitting, or rather crouching, against a rude stone bench, which serves as an anvil, and as one, with practised hand,

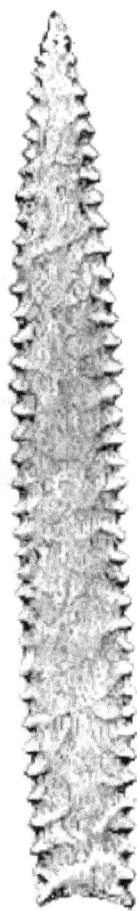

Knife and saw of the late Stone Age.

splits flake after flake from a fine block of flint (please observe that she gives just three strokes, and directs these at as many different angles of the flake to be detached), the other takes them up and goes on to smooth and grind and polish them on one of those curious rounded polishing stones beside you, and you

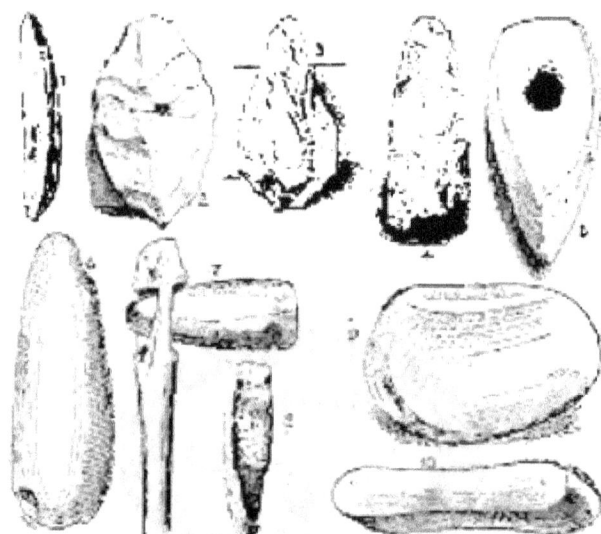

Palæolithic Flint Working.—1. Flint flake.   2. Flint core.
3. Flint weapon.
Neolithic Implements.—4. Stone celt, partly ground. 5. Stone
axe-hammer. 6. Polished celt. 7. Mounted celt. 8. Stone
knife set in staghorn handle. 9, 10. Grinding and polishing
stones.—(From the British Museum: about ⅓ natural size.)

see hatchet, awl, and chisel, finished off in quick succession, and laid aside ready for use.   With the flint core itself a lance head may be made.   Arrow heads of every kind, sling-stones, scrapers, celts, and a score of other objects are here in abundance, and a heap of chips and broken flakes in the corner tell us that an abortive stroke or a flaw in the flint are occurrences not altogether unknown.

Behind this pair a man is employed in modelling a clumsy vessel of some kind. He squats on the floor, legs outspread, and on the ground before him he has a mass of coarse reddish clay, which he tries to work into some sort of shape. It is a poor affair when done, but he surveys it with no small satisfaction, and goes on to ornament it by pinching the edges with finger and thumb, and still further by passing pieces of cord round

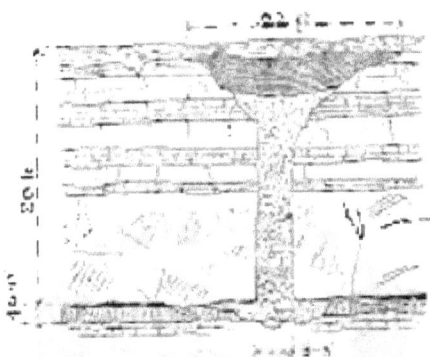

Pre-historic Flint Mine.

it at intervals, tying the ends of each, and then slightly drawing them together so as to produce a series of irregular rings. The baking is very imperfect, for he knows nothing of ovens, so that these utensils are very soon rendered *hors de combat*.

But these shrewd artisans have discovered that flint taken direct from its native bed is easier to work and vastly superior in every way to the blocks picked up by the roadside. So I can now show you a veritable flint-mine—one of many [1] in the neighbourhood—

[1] Canon Greenwell found one at Brandon, in Suffolk, which contained 254 shafts.

worked by the men before you. It has eight shafts in
the face of a layer of limestone eighty-one feet long.
These open out at the top like funnels, and the flint
has been struck at little over three feet below the
surface. The shafts are in some cases continued by
galleries or by trenches, and though the light is rather
bad owing to numerous little landslips you can plainly
see the floor, for it is trodden hard by the feet of the
primeval miner. The practical knowledge displayed is

Dwelling of the Stone Age.

wonderful. Here the flint has been left standing in
pillars at frequent intervals; there they have propped
up the galleries with some other stable material,
cemented with clay. They are not able always to prevent landslips, however, for every now and then you see a
staghorn tool flattened by the fall of a gallery roof.
The marks of the prehistoric picks are everywhere
visible, and indeed more than once you come across a
tool still embedded in the rock, just as the miner left it.

The commoner neolithic dwelling itself is not much
better than those we have already seen, but the race

c 2

has increased and multiplied according to the custom
of races ever after, and, like a good many other people
you may have heard of, they begin to find that there
isn't positively elbow room for them in the old place, so

Núragh of Zuri.

they turn out to do for themselves, and set up house-
keeping on their own account in those huts entirely
built of boulders, or roofed over with branches, mud,
and grass, and which they can erect wherever their
fancy may lead them.   The sites are all one price, and

the game laws no more stringent in one place than
another; in short, the choice is unlimited. By and by,
when the old folks, their fathers, pop off, it is too much
trouble to return to the ancestral roof, and the family
plate is not worth squabbling about, so the hyena and
other old tenants take advantage of the situation to
sneak back to their original quarters, and settle them-

Doorway and niche of Nûragh.

selves down once more ! This time they have undisputed possession.

But although the mud-built hut is the prevailing
style of habitation, it is not the only one. In that part
of our street which after ages will call Sardinia there
are thousands of immense structures of unmortared
stone; all the homes of the later stone men. Shaped
like truncated cones, they have one, two, or even three

Talayot.　(Balearic Isles.)

rooms, one above another; a winding stair, formed of
huge boulders placed in the thickness of the wall lead-

ing from the lower to the upper chambers. In the thickness of the wall there are also two or three niches constructed as hiding places, and one is always placed to the right of the door as a lurking place for the defender of the entrance in time of attack. The oldest of these dwellings (known afterwards as "Nuraghi") have only one great room with an arched roof. In the Balearic Isles these cyclopean piles are called "Talayoti," and in the island of Pantellaria, "Sesi." In Caledonia there are hundreds of them called "Burghs," while the

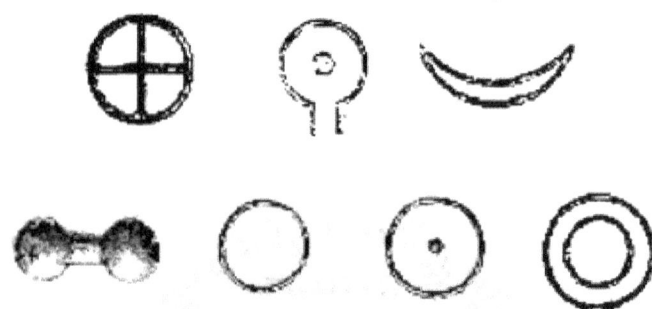

Ring-cross ; Sun and Moon Signs.

Fort of Staigue at Kerry is another, but less ancient example.

It may be rather a morbid taste, but I confess I have quite as much interest in the abodes of the dead as in those of the living, and if I did not show you the sepulchres of the Men of Bone, it was because their houses during life became their tombs at death ; there was therefore nothing different to show. Now, however, the disposal of the dead is quite a feature of the time. As civilization advances, the vague religious instincts inherent in even the most primitive human mind take a more defined form, and find expression in signs and symbols, which, long before they are deemed applicable to every-day life, are employed in connection with funeral rites and ceremonies. The worship of

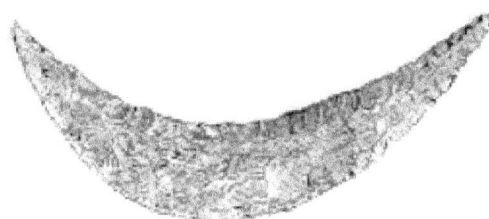

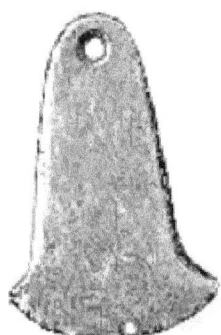

1. Crescent Knife.   2. Hammer.   3. Axe Amulet.

Neolithic Dolmen.

ancestors and of natural forces, or rather of that great
source of all force—the sun—are no doubt the earliest

religions of our prehistoric parents, and the ring-cross

by which they represented the sun is carved on nearly all their tombs, sometimes on every separate stone of these. The moon is usually shown by a cup-shaped hollow, or a simple ring, with or without a dot in the centre, but those finely chipped crescent-shaped flints prove that every phase of the fair goddess has been studied. The mighty god of thunder is specially invoked, and the axe and hammer are his attributes, so great quantities of these, generally made of amber and quite small in size, are included in the outfit of a dead Stone Age warrior. The tombs vary a good deal in

Giant's Tomb. (La Mormors.)

form, here are three of them, and their names—"Dolmen," "Cromlech," and "Menhir"—meaning "stone table," "stone circle" and "long stone," express their appearance very well. Sometimes the dolmen has raised over it an immense mound of earth; this is a "tumulus," or covered dolmen, and is common enough in some places. In these graves the bodies are generally laid in a crouching position, with knees drawn up and arms crossed on the breast, and very rarely indeed will you find any evidence of cremation.

Now I will trouble you to move on, please; we can't stand here talking about wild beasts and savages. On our right a much superior individual is waiting to be introduced. Stand back! Oh ye proud devisers of all manner of marvels—ye who rip up the bowels of your mother, that ye may find wherewith to feed your furnaces and fill your cauldrons! Bare your heads and uncover your feet, for surely those who stand silent but eloquent before you, half naked, unkempt uncouth, are yet worthy of highest honour—honour most of all from you who have been their disciples, through all the ages since they laid down their tools. Think for a moment of the time and circumstances in which these men lived and laboured: think of the obstacles they overcame, and the works they have left behind them; and then say if you grudge them their meed of praise— for, reader, we have arrived at the age of Bronze!

Behold the first metallurgist!

The First Metallurgist.

CHAPTER II

MEN OF METAL

BUT although you are no doubt satisfied to hob-nob with such distinguished gentlemen as those last referred to, you need not imagine that you will be able to give our good friends of the stone age the slip in this abrupt and heartless manner. Not at all!

Throughout the entire age of bronze, and even during part of that of iron, flint weapons are used, and used pretty extensively too by the poorer part of the community, who can't afford to keep up with this expensive fad of their betters; for as yet the art of working in metal is not by any means known to everybody. The lucky few who have acquired it to take care to keep the monopoly. They are looked upon as something not very canny by their less enlightened neighbours, who can only attribute their wonderful skill to magical arts, and who, while quite willing to profit by these, are considerably chary about coming into actual contact with the magicians themselves.

Just watch that great fellow skulking round the house, will you? He is evidently bent on some mysterious errand, and though it is a rather dark night, you can see that he carries a large bundle under one arm and has a smaller flat packet in his hand. You think, of course, that he has been on a little predatory excursion. Quite a mistake, I can assure you. He is only making his way to the abode of one of those awful beings who keep the beautiful new weapons for which his soul longs, and he carries with him the piece of deer's flesh which he considers a fair price for the object he desires to possess. Now he has reached the workshop door, and with a stealthy glance round he uncovers a fine haunch, hangs it up just by the aperture, and, with a sharp piece of bone, fastens to it the little flat object, which is nothing less than a very carefully cut-out pattern of the particular shape he prefers for his spear head (you observe that it is a leaf he has used for this purpose); then he glides off as secretly as he came—and that is all for the present.

But if you should be here again to-morrow night you will see the second part of the transaction. Another midnight visit will be made to the same shrine, where the coveted weapon will, most likely, be found ready, replacing the joint behind the door. If it be made entirely to the buyer's satisfaction, a second offering of flesh may perhaps find its way to the same pot. Oh, yes! They are fully aware of the value of the discovery they have made, are these men of metal, and know well enough how to maintain their own importance. Cornering is by no means a new game you will observe.

There is very little chance of our being permitted to inspect the bronze-smith's foundry[1] in a fair and square sort of way, so we must content ourselves with what the chinks in the wall reveal. Now, would you believe it, the old gentleman has had another visitor this dark night—and a highly favoured one, too, it appears, for she has been admitted into the sanctum, and is present at the very incantation itself. Yes, I said she. These high-falutin priests of bronze are no more proof against a woman's eyes than the most of us; and here we have this enterprising young lady not only wheedling our friend into making all manner of personal ornaments

---

[1] Smith and founder were one in those days.

for her, but actually insisting on seeing how they are
made. She wears a very handsome necklace of jet, but

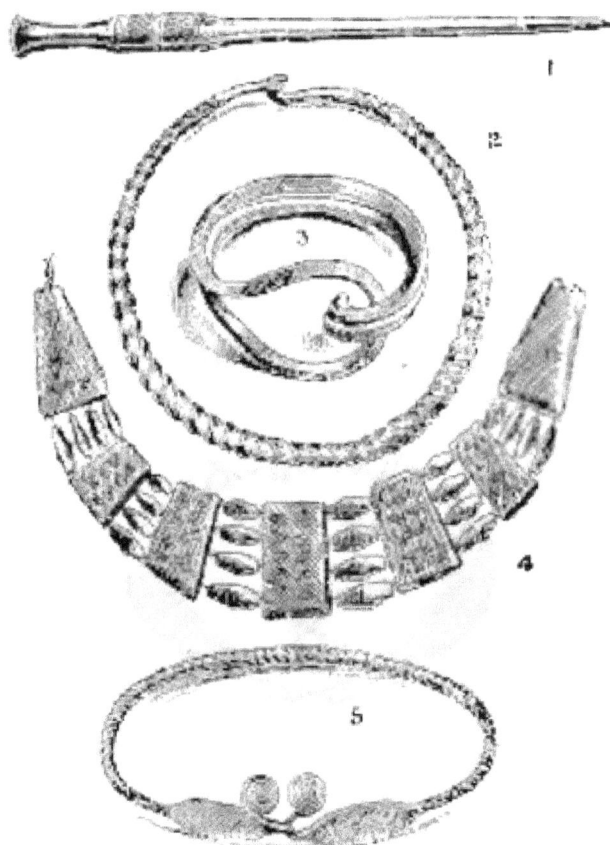

Personal ornaments of the Bronze Age. 1. Bronze hair-pin (½).
2. Bronze torc, for the neck (¼). 3. Bronze bracelet (½).
4. Jet necklace. 5. Bronze diadem (½). (British Museum.)

the torc, or collar of bronze this elderly lover of hers
bestows, is evidently much more to her mind, and her

satisfaction is complete when he crowns her with this quaint bronze diadem. What a chance to set the whole hamlet of girls crazy with envy!

While she surveys her new finery, we may glance round the shop. The walls are burnt black, as in a furnace, and against them are piled nearly two tons of

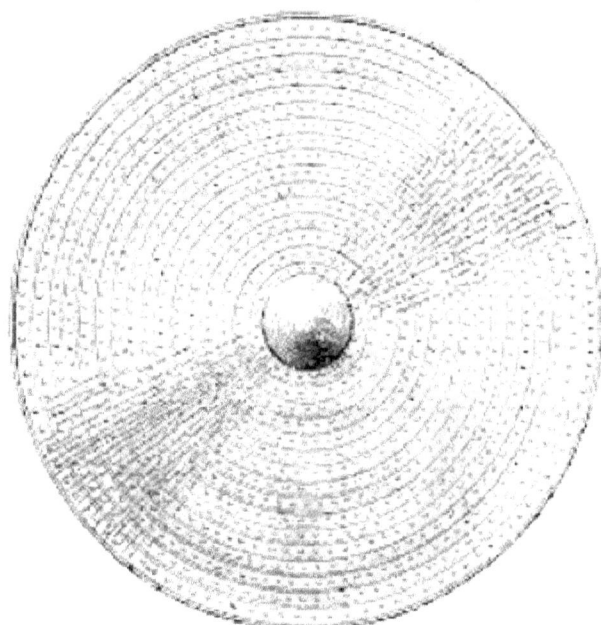

Bronze Shield, in repoussé (⅖). (British Museum.)

bronze, partly in lumps, partly in slabs, and old hatchets, swords and daggers, intended for re-casting. The place is quite an armoury, and the weapons are in many cases very beautiful. What can be finer than that circular shield in repoussé, for instance? Here are two or three types of axes: this one is solid, mounted in a split stick, and firmly bound by strong wire. Another has been cast hollow, and hafted on a stick which exactly fits the hollow. It has a little loop of metal cast upon it also, which is used in tying

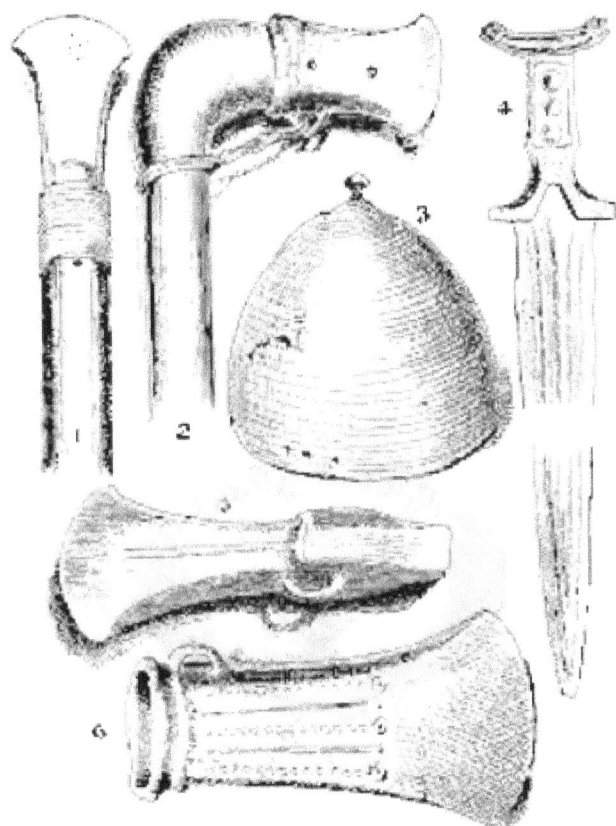

Bronze Weapons. 1. Method of hafting solid celt with split stick (⅔). 2. Method of casting hollow celt (½). 3. Helmet (⅓). 4. Sword, with hollow handle riveted on (½); blade, 30 ins. 5. Solid celt (⅔). 6. Hollow celt (½). (British Museum.)

the celt to the handle with wire. Of course, these various types necessitate various methods of casting. In some cases single, and in others double moulds of

loam, stone, or metal, are used; whilst a third, and
perhaps the commonest method, is to encase a wooden
or waxen model in loam, which on exposure to heat is
burnt out, leaving a cavity for the reception of the
molten metal.

You will however become acquainted with the bronze
people best by examining their handiwork as applied
to sacred objects. With higher cultivation, a corre-

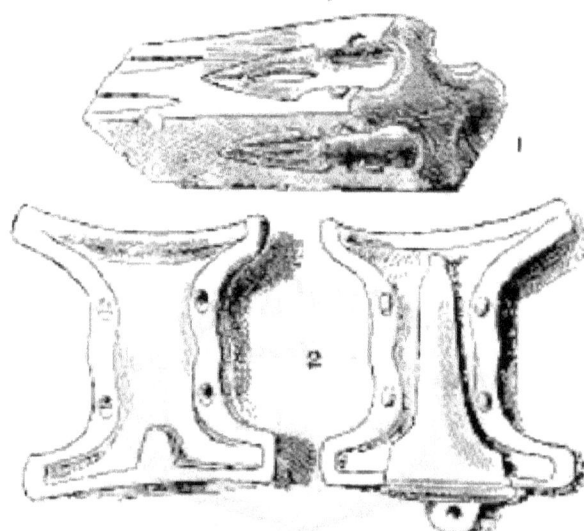

Stone half-mould for various spear-points (½).   2. Pair of
bronze moulds for sword handle, with core piece to give the
hollow (¼).   (British Museum.)

spondingly increased religious feeling prevails, and the
belief in a future existence is everywhere shown by the
care with which the departing soul is fitted out for its
long and weary journey. The sacred symbols of the
men of stone have both developed in character and increased in number. The ring-cross has become the
wheel-cross, for the sun is now believed to drive across
the sky in a chariot, an idea which causes the horse to

become one of the sacred animals. Zig-zag flashes of
lightning too have suggested the sun-snake, which
is now the special emblem of fertility. I could show
you all manner of variations on the ring-cross and wheel-
cross as well as on the snake curve ; a very few must
suffice for to-day, yet in those, you can see that
already some notion of a divine trinity has been
conceived. The "Swastika"
is a development of the sun-
snake, and the origin of
spiral ornament. The stars
too have taken their place in
the prehistoric pantheon, and
the sacred ship, a hitherto
unknown emblem, now figures
on nearly all articles having a

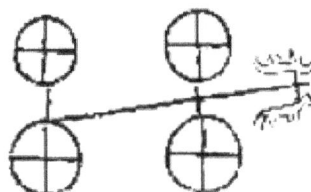

Son-god's chariot.

religious purpose. Here is one of the most beautiful
objects used by the Bronze Chief in his temple. It is
the horn or trumpet with which he is accustomed to
call his tribe to worship, and perhaps also he adores

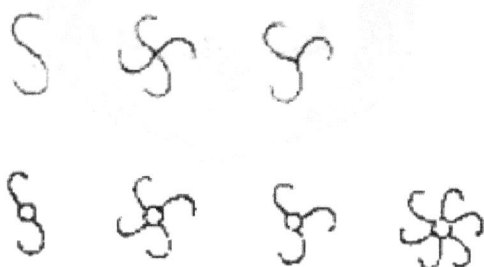

"Bar-snake."   "Swastika."   "Triskele."   "Star-sign."

his God with a blast imitative of the awful thunder
peal, and peculiarly acceptable on that account. Upon
it you can discern quite a number of Bronze-Age
symbols. But there are two or three others I am
anxious to show you, because you will come across some

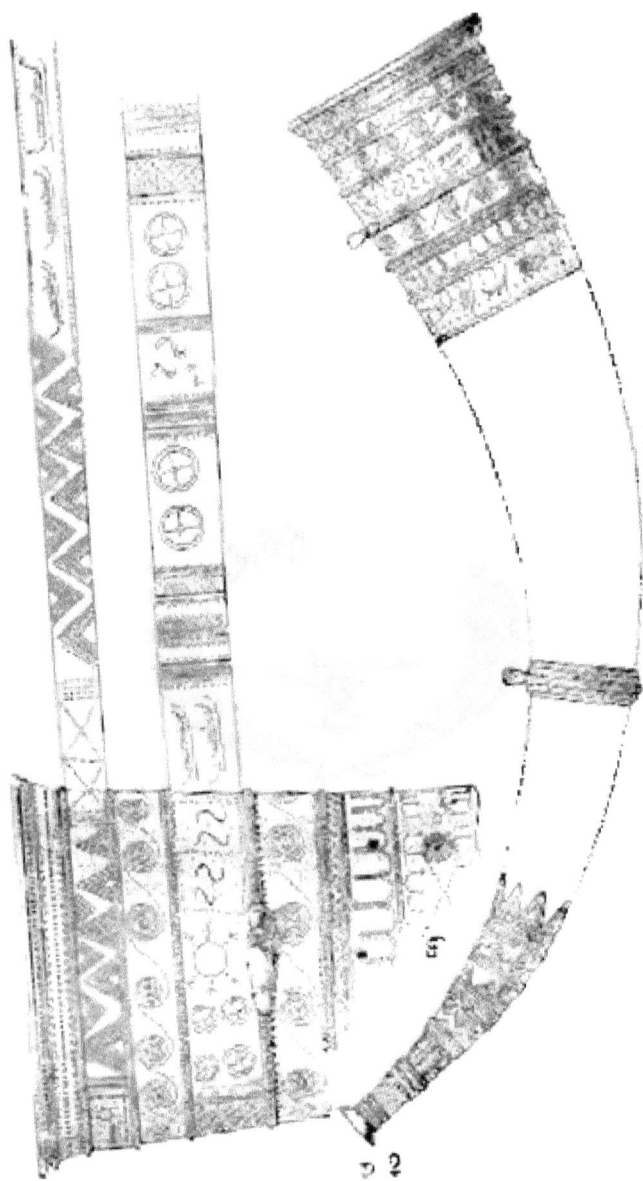

Bronze horn from the bog of Wismar.

of them many times as you ascend our street. The first
is a bird with a long bill - a goose, in fact—and I have

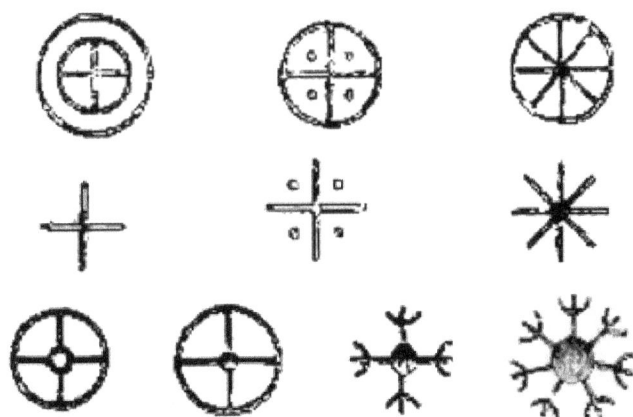

Variations on ring and wheel cross.

seen a very graceful hanging vase or sacrificial vessel
of which this sign forms a conspicuous ornament. A
bird is, among other things,
typical of motion, and is
generally used where mo-
tion is implied, about the
sun for instance, or at the
prow of a boat. A second
prevailing symbol is the
stag, and particularly the
horns, which, placed on the
head of a figure, always
denotes divinity. This
horned helmet is worn by
the priest in yonder pagan
temple, and beside it is a
wooden figure of the deity he worships.

Sun-disc with sacred
ship and horse.

The women of the bronze villages hold a much higher

position than did their stone-age sisters, possibly because the adoration of the moon has brought female deities into vogue. At any rate the most beautiful little daggers and shields are now made for them, and they have now begun to bear their husbands and fathers company on many an exciting hunting expedition. You will be greatly interested in seeing the actual wearing apparel of these ancient dames. This is

Hanging-vessel from a bog in Fanoe.

a complete costume, prepared, alas, as a shroud for a lady high in authority here. The long woollen skirt, and jacket with its sleeves all in one piece, are remarkably well made, and the girdle and artistic cap or net for the hair would not disgrace people a long way further up the street. Besides these, she will wear a bronze head-ring, a pair of bracelets, and two spiral finger-rings.

But here is a little group of dwellings which must by no means be overlooked as we traverse this street of human habitations. They cannot lay claim to an epoch exclusively their own, it is true; for evidences of stone and bronze are distributed in fairly equal proportions among them, whilst some even bespeak an acquaintance with iron; but they are not the less interesting on that account, and are by far the most picturesque of all the dwellings of prehistoric times. Indeed it is equally mislead-

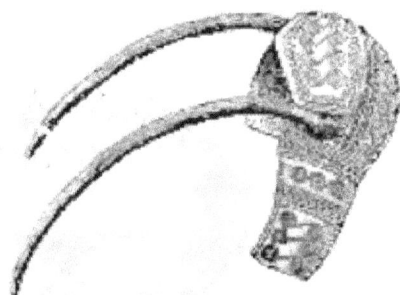

Horned god and horned helmet of Bronze Age.

Human feet and moon signs, stored in the Bronze Age.

ing to confine them either to time or place. You are now looking at the habitations of prehistoric Switzerland, but eastwards, in Thrace, is a lake city of considerably later growth. And a very thriving com-

Costume of a Bronze Age lady.

munity it is; for every time a man helps himself to a
wife, he is compelled to bring three posts from the sur-
rounding forests and set them up in the lake; and as
no restriction whatever is placed on the number of
wives he may take, the city grows and flourishes
amazingly.

The Crannoges of Ireland are precisely like these pile
dwellings, though built long after them, and at the
very top of our street are many similar erections, the
homes of men who even now are passing through their

Lake dwelling.

stone and bronze apprenticeship. The village before
you is, as you see, erected on a platform of logs, which
is supported on piles driven into the bottom of the
lake before you, and, as someone facetiously remarks,
they look more suitable to a colony of ducks than
human beings. The huts themselves are built of logs,
branches, and rushes, and usually plastered inside
with mud. The burnt-out boat is an indispensable
adjunct to such a dwelling, and, together with this draw-
bridge of logs, affords ample means of access to the
shore.

I think we might do worse than cross the bridge and

peep into one of these watery strongholds. What a
menagerie it is! Horses, sheep, dogs, cows, goats,
pigs; and all quite as much at home as the lord of
the manor himself. The children are stretched at full
length outside,—the very little ones fastened with
cords to prevent their falling into the water—and have
apparently been fishing over the edge of the platform
for their supper, and are now having a grand scrimmage about an immense pike which has just been
caught. Fish is so abundant in the lake that it is

1. Pottery of the Bronze Age (⅓). 2. Bronze
cauldron (⅓). (British Museum.)

only necessary to dip a basket into the water and
bring it up full; and almost every house has a trap-
door in the middle of the floor, by means of which the
fishing may proceed in all sorts of weather. Excellent
nets too are made by these people, who have learnt
not only to weave but to tan. The women are bruising
and grinding corn, mending nets, baking cake, and
spinning flax, inside. There is a stone hearth in the
middle of the floor, and along one side of the apartment are ranged quite a dozen very large pottery jars.
It will amuse you to look into them, for they represent

the wardrobes, store-closets, and jewel-cases of the entire household. The first contains a quantity of woollen garments belonging to the youngsters; next comes an assortment of toilet necessaries, hairpins,

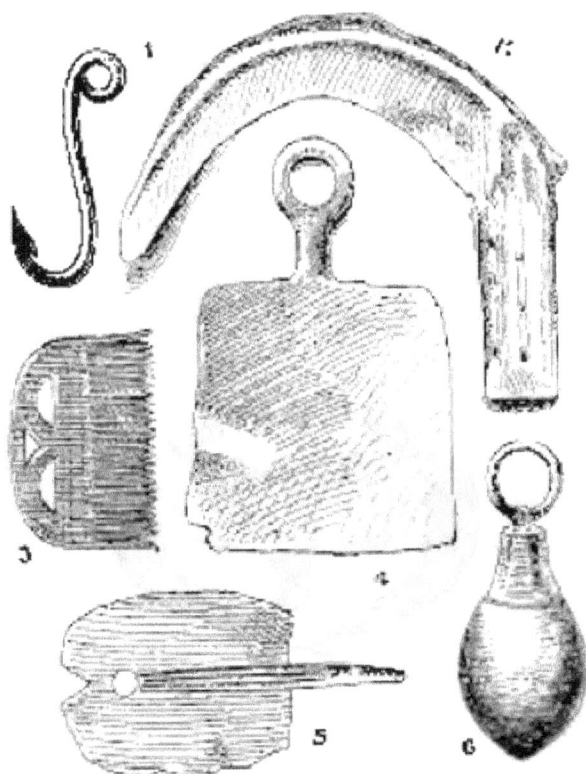

Bronze implements. 1. Fish-hook (⅘) 2. Sickle (⅓) 3. Comb (⅓). 4, 5. Razor knives (⅓) 6. Bell (⅓) (British Museum.)

razors—oh, such razors!—combs, and tweezers. The third is full of apples, cut in quarters and dried ready for winter. Further on you come to stores of nuts, leaves, barley, wheat, linen clothing, and an endless

supply of bronze weapons. Altogether you must admit
that these bronze-age housewives are a very thrifty
and orderly set of women. But those remarkable
semicircular and hollowed-out objects of pottery
against the opposite wall are puzzling you, I see.
They are simply head rests, sir, and if you look
again at the fearful and wonderful methods of hair-
dressing which the ladies affect, their use will become quite apparent. One can see with half an eye
that many an hour has been spent in the erection of
these indescribable coiffures, for they are meant to last,

Danish tumulus (after Lubbock).

let me tell you; hence the impossibility of lying down
without some such protection as the articles over there
can give.

However, we are invited to a highly important ceremony to-night, so let us bid adieu to these pleasant
dwellers on marsh and lake, and take our places near
that piece of rising ground opposite. A long, mournful
procession is slowly winding round the side of the hill,
and approaches the spot where you stand. You perceive there is an opening in the side of the mound, and
that the latter is hollow—in fact a tomb. A glance
inside shows you two coffins already there; one a very

Garments from the Treenhoi tumulus.

tiny one; and you are here to see the house of the dead receive its third and last occupant. The babe has slept there for many a day: the mother but for a few moons, and now the father comes to rest beside them, and not again for long ages will that silent family be disturbed. He is the chief of his race and the last of his kin, so he must be buried with fitting honours, and in the ancient manner of his forefathers too, though with the majority of the bronze folk inhumation is now out of fashion; cremation is quite the order of the day.

Right in front of you the bearers halt and lay their burden down; then they begin, in presence of all his people, to attire him for his long sojourn in the spirit land. First of all a woollen shirt is slipped over his head. It is nicely hollowed out at the neck, and altogether very well shaped. Somebody hands a long woollen strap with which to bind it at the waist; they pass it twice round and tie it loosely in front. Then a pair of woollen leggings are drawn on to the stiffened limbs, and boots of half-tanned leather cover the feet. A large semicircular cloak comes next, which you may fasten with a bronze brooch, and on the inner side of this cloak a number of short woollen threads are left hanging, which give it something of the appearance of plush.

On the head now place that hemispherical cap; it is very thick, and the outside is covered with the same short threads as are on the cloak, only in this case each thread has a curious little knot at the end. Over all an ox-hide, and your work is nearly done. Here is his coffin: an immense one it is, measuring nine feet eight inches long, and two feet two inches wide: made of wood, with a movable lid, and certainly rather rough, but he will sleep none the less soundly in it for all that. Roll this long, fringed shawl into a pillow, and lay him down with his head upon it. A similar shawl you spread over his feet, and close to his hand place these

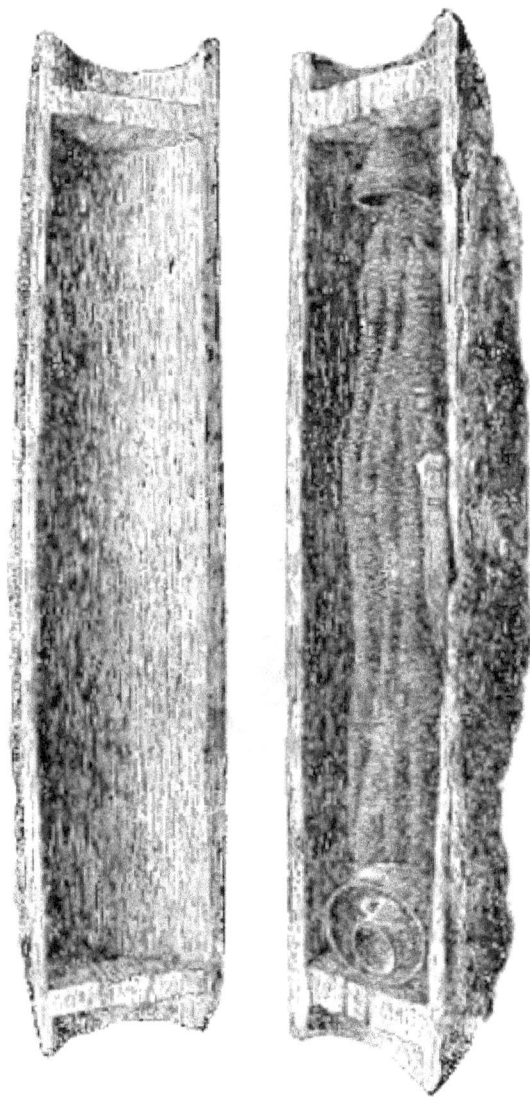

Oak coffin of the Early Iron Age.

objects you think he prizes most ; all his little toilet
appurtenances — a bone comb and rude razor-knife ; a
pair of bronze tweezers ; a large double stud and some
tin buttons. Besides these, give him his favourite
weapons ; spear and arrow head, sword and dagger, all
of bronze ; some fish hooks, a gouge and small saw,
as well as a stone hammer ; and now I think he is
very well equipped, so you may put on the lid and help

Sacrificial knives.

to carry him in to the place reserved for him in that
chamber of everlasting repose. The people have still
their orgies of dancing and singing to go through, on
the top of this same hill, round the fire they have lit
and the stone they have set up in honour of their
departed chief, but your part in the proceedings is
over.

Do you want to see what is left of the great man
ages after this night's performance is forgotten, and

when the actors in it have passed into oblivion? Suppose you close your eyes for a moment and then open them again in the year of our Lord 1861. You have leaped over a chasm of something like three thousand years: perhaps a great deal more; and you find yourself on a little farm in Jutland, and once more before that open grave—they call it the Tumulus of Treenhoi now. The garments are nearly as perfect as when you saw them placed there: the weapons too, are unchanged; but the man himself? Ah! for flesh you have only this dark greasy substance, embedded in which is a sort of blue powder, which has once been bone. The brain alone remains undecayed. It lies on the pillow just where you left it, and is covered by the same woollen cap; but for the case which then held it, you look in vain.

The mother's coffin has nothing to give us, except a little dust perhaps; from the baby's we take the tiny bronze bracelet that once encircled the dear little pink arm; a smooth, round stone ball; and one poor little amber bead!

But the age of bronze gives way to that of iron. The smeltor of copper and tin is superseded by the skilled worker in a newer metal, one whose potentialities are inexhaustible, and whose value to man can never be overestimated, one that is to lift him a higher rung on the ladder of civilization than any he has yet reached, or ever could have reached, so far as we can see, without it.

CHAPTER III.

In the early days of the iron age you will not find much attention paid to architecture. The houses are neater and more workmanlike than those of preceding epochs; but they are still very primitive, built of logs

Dwelling of the Iron Age.

and thatched with straw, and resembling nothing so much as the rustic arbours to be seen in the grounds at most country seats of the present day. But in all evidences of knowledge and culture, the iron folk far outstrip those who have come before them. The little patch that you now see before each dwelling is carefully cultivated, and tells much of the industry and method of the people. In Spring you may see plough and harrow at work in those tidy fields behind, and in Autumn the sickle is no less busy.

Here is the smithy with its roaring furnace, its clanging anvil, and its everlasting clatter and din. Further along you have the wood-yard and can hear the rasping of the saw, and count the short sharp strokes of axe and hatchet. In the next cottage the women are busy at their weaving frames, and the merry click-clack, click-clack, goes on all through the

Primitive blast furnaces.

long drowsy afternoon. Ah! I thought so; the smithy door has an irresistible attraction; you positively cannot pass it by. Well, you may stop a minute and compare it with the last I showed you. As I told you before, in archæological matters, you cannot be off with the old love before you are on with the new, and as you found many a stone weapon among a bronze-working community, so you see bronze ornaments in abundance before you now. But they are ornaments only, iron being now the favourite metal for weapons and cutting-tools. Unlike their predecessors, the iron men are not at all averse to having their methods examined, for you see them here fashioning their weapons in the most public manner, and over yonder they are preparing new metal from the ore. What do you think of their blast-furnace? Ingenious, is it not? The ore and fuel are piled up in the centre, and those extraordinary-looking inflated goat-skins are the bellows. If you watch the workmen for a moment, you will quite understand the *modus operandi*. Each man is provided with a pair of skins, the leg apertures being tightly tied up, while that at the neck is open to allow of inflation. As one foot is pressed down the other is raised, and simultaneously the collapsed bellows is pulled open by a cord, so that the two skins are emptied and filled alternately—a very good contrivance indeed, you must admit, for men at this early time of day; and if we had a little more time, I could show you another furnace not very far off, where two tunnels pierce a mound, being wide at the west side whence blows a

Woollen trousers of the Age of Iron, with combined stockings. (*Engelhardt.*)

strong wind, and tapering until they emerge, very narrow, on the opposite side, where the fire is placed and blown by this strong, natural draught. And yet another furnace, cone-shaped and made of clay, sus-

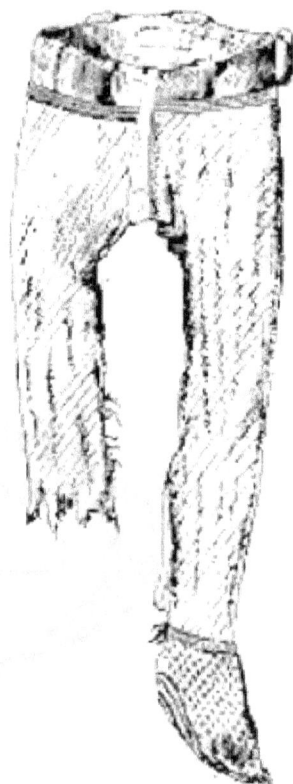

R 2

picionaly like one built by people near the top of our street, among the Pyrenees in Catalonia. I daresay you know these later workmen: they have had some 3000 years of metallurgical experience since the goat-skin bellows-workers set the headline to the copy-book, and the main principles have not changed so very much after all.

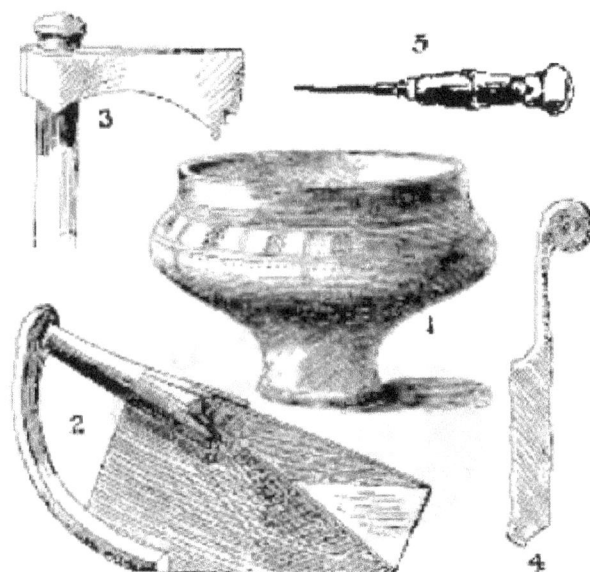

Tools and domestic utensils of the Iron Age. 1. Earthen-ware cooking vessel (½). 2. Wooden scoop (⅟₁₀). 3. Iron axe (⅜). 4. Iron knife (½). 5. Awl with wooden handle (½). (Engelhardt.)

But the iron men realize just as much as you, that " all work and no play makes Jack a dull boy," and as a matter of fact, there is hardly one of them to be seen just now. They are all off to a neighbouring hamlet where games are being held on a somewhat extensive scale. They have left the women at home; but these

are no doubt accustomed to a certain amount of conjugal
neglect, and are amusing themselves fairly well, notwithstanding. They know not the delight of the social
rubber, but at draughts neither you nor I would stand
much chance with them; and these dice bear pretty
strong evidence that games of chance are also in high
favour. However, they do not leave their household

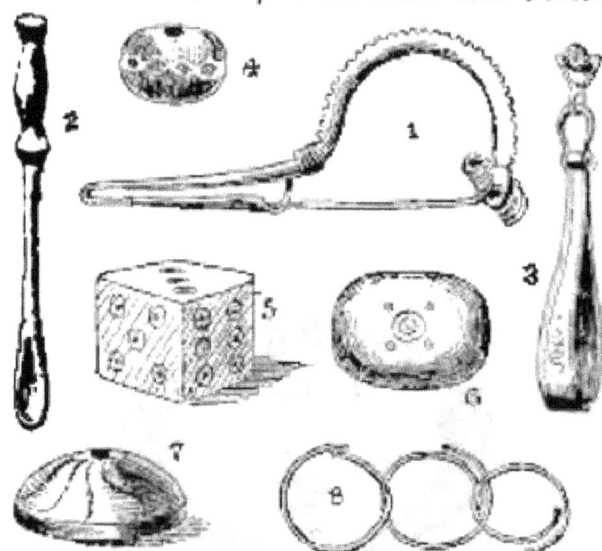

Trinkets, &c., of the Iron Age. 1. Bronze fibula or brooch (¼).
2. Silver ear-pick (½). 3. Bronze tweezers (½). 4. Glass
bead (½). 5. 6 Bronze and amber dice (½). 7. Glass button
(½. 8. Gold ring money (½). (Engraved.)

duties undone ; here is a pair of trousers—rather the
worse for wear, it is true—but proving that the quality
of these good women's handiwork is far ahead of that
shown by the woollen garments of Treenhoi. Their
cooking vessels, too, are most artistic (more like draw-
ing-room ornaments than kitchen kettles), while their
trinkets — bow-shaped brooches or fibulæ of bronze, beads

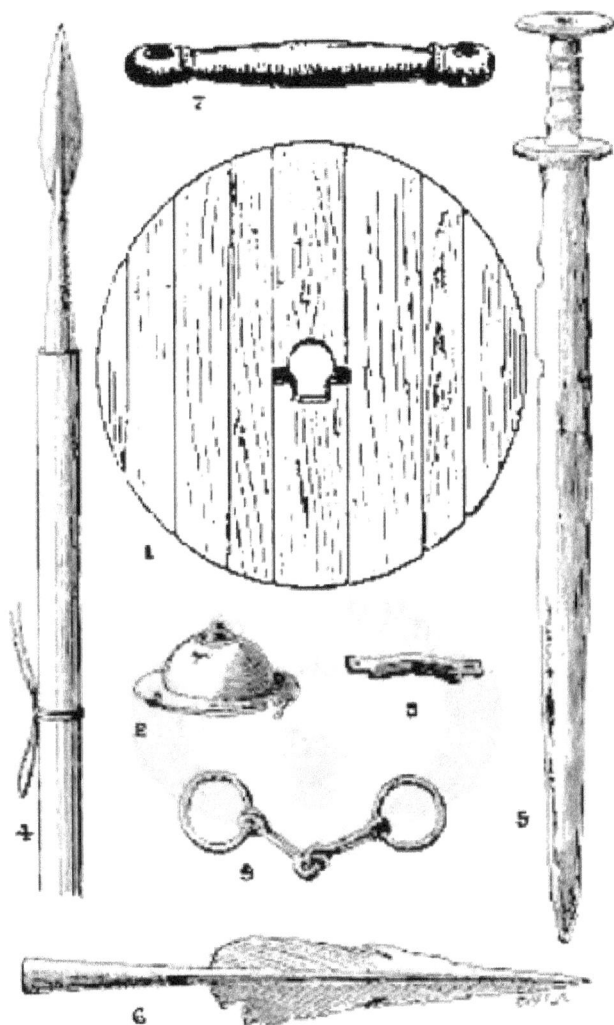

Accoutrements in wood and iron. 1. Wooden shield (⅟₇).
2. Bronze boss for shield (⅝). 3. Wooden handle of Shield (⅓).
4. Iron javelin with casting cord (⅓). 5. Iron sword with
bone handle (⅓). 6. Leaf-shaped lance-head in iron (⅔).
7. Bronze horse-bit (¼). 8. Iron bit with snaffle rings.
(Engelhardt.)

and buttons of glass, tweezers and earpicks of silver—betoken a large amount of skill on the part of the artificers, and no little dandyism on the part of the wearers.

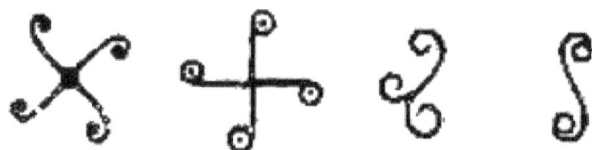

Sacred symbols of the Iron Age.

Silver Brooch of "Swastika" or double Sun-snake form.

Let us look at the armoury. Here are some wonderful examples of the metal-worker's art, and we shall soon see that with increased excellence in the manufacture of weapons, there has also come to be much greater occasion to use them. War is a recognized in-

stitution and fighting men a necessity. But you
cannot understand, and for the
life of me I cannot tell you,
why these iron warriors should
possess such exquisitely-formed
swords, lances, and spears of
metal, and yet content themselves with shields like this
miserable wooden thing which
you have doubtless mistaken
for the lid of a copper all the
time.

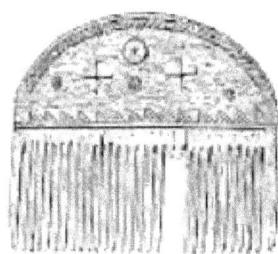

Bone Comb decorated with
the " Swastika " and
other sacred symbols.

The development in the
sacred signs is unmistakable.

Earthen Jar of the Northern Iron Age.

The straight-armed swastika and triskele have not yet
appeared; the curved forms are all-prevailing. This

silver brooch is an excellent example of the swastika, but such a favourite has this design become that the commonest articles are now decorated with it. The bull is the acknowledged emblem of the God of Thunder,

Gold-plated ornament from Coat of Mail.

and the bolts which the iron folk believe to fall during storms, are the teeth which the heavenly creature spits out in his fury. The ornamentation of the earthen vessel at your side shows that the human foot of Bronze Age origin is still regarded as a sacred symbol. But here

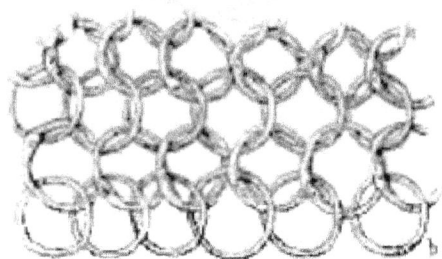

Coat of Mail from the bogs of Denmark.

is an object which will fully occupy your attention any
time you have half an hour to spare. It is a round
ornament detached from the coat of mail lying near,
and the longer you examine it, the more do you find in

Iron Age Amulets or Bracteates of gold.

it to study. Every imaginable sign and symbol of a
sacred nature is lavishly inscribed—most of them quite
regardless of order or design, I must admit ; however,
the warrior who wears this on his breast, should certainly
be protected from perils of earth, air and sea, if the

gods thereof have anything to say in the matter. I must not forget to show you some of the lovely golden bracteates or amulets which are the latest fashion with the ladies of this period; replacing the little bone discs and amber hammers of their grandmothers. You can follow the patterns for yourself; the various devices ought to be familiar to you by now. That silver goblet, too, will bear inspection. The horse is still sacred to the sun, but is far too useful now-a-days to be devoted solely to religious purposes. In these troublous times the iron warrior rides to battle on steeds as richly caparisoned as himself. The bits and chains are beautifully worked in bronze and mounted with gold and silver, and bronze spurs with iron points are among the newest accoutrements of the rider himself.

Silver Goblet.

But who are these who sweep across the plain? Are they the truant sons and husbands? Are they the victors from the arena, bearing home the wonderful lump of iron that has been the most coveted prize to-day? The shrieks of defenceless women tell you it is none of these; a treacherous tribe is bearing down on the unhappy village with murder and plunder in every gesture. For one moment the women are paralyzed, and the next an exceeding bitter cry breaks from each as she realizes the doom that awaits her. Then the iron hearts are braced, the iron nerves controlled. The fair young daughter of the absent chief comes forth,

Bronze Bit, the ends of the chains mounted in gold and silver.

summons the workmen together, and places each at the head of a dozen desperate women. The old grandsire, too feeble now to win laurels in the arena, and whose mantle has long been transferred to the shoulders of his son, is hurried from his couch of soft skins. Sword and shield are given him, and as if the very touch of them carried the elixir of life back to his stagnant veins, he stands, with form erect and flashing eye, before that little army, and takes once more a chieftain's place among them. On rushes that terrible charge, confident but careless, for what can a score or two of women do to meet the attack of a hundred reckless men? Well, let them boast, and let them come;

they have yet to learn what women can and will do for home and honour. In front of the closely built huts the old chief arranges his lines, three deep in the centre, and flanked by short columns nine deep, forming three sides of a square. They are but a handful alto-

Spur of an Iron Age warrior.

gether, but they make the best of their resources, and besides the protection of the walls behind, they receive considerable advantage from the trees which outline their side wings. Three minutes more, and the traitors are on them. A shower of spears speed from the unfamiliar hands within the square, carrying death among those who little expected such a reception; but the repulse is only momentary, and the devoted little band suffers fearfully in its turn. First this side, and then the other, has the advantage, and alas! more than one absent warrior is already wifeless or motherless. Now the enemy has abandoned unsatisfactory skirmishing, and sets itself the task of deciding the day by the destruction of the leader. The latter fights

for the remnant of his army with the fierceness of
despair; he parries a thrust here and another there;
sends every moment another and another messenger of
Death into the ranks before him. Again and again
the weight of the javelins which pierce his wooden
shield render the latter too heavy for him to support,
and as often some faithful hand passes him a fresh one,
her own life being given with it. But he cannot hold
on much longer. Already he has done a herculean

Funeral Pyre of an Iron chief.

task; the spirit is brave as ever, but the fictitious
strength is all but spent. Listen! a cry of horror
rings the air as home from their revels speed the
laggards at last. What a home-coming! Vengeance
is all that is left them, and they take their fill of it.
Of that goodly company which came so gaily over the
plains this morning, not one shall make the backward
journey. There is a perfect carnival of blood, but not
for long. In ten minutes a mangled heap and a dozen
prisoners are all that remain of the would-be
plunderers. But the last of them has done his work

Damascened Sword, with Scabbard.

only too well, and has sent the heroic old chieftain to his long sleep with a javelin in his heart.

You have seen the funeral of a Bronze Age warrior. Now I will show you how they honour one of the Iron age. His funeral pyre is filled with corpses and shrieking prisoners; his well-worn sword and battered shield and helmet are placed with him upon the summit, a rich brooch adorns his breast; a ring of gold lies on his nerveless hand: and amid the wails of his adoring people he passes into the Silent Land.

But come, let us make one more ghostly journey together, before we bid adieu to a people who were in their zenith before the first historian on this side of the street thought of recording deeds of man or fate of nations. This time we will alight among the bogs of Sleswick, and beside

the one known as the Moss of Nydam. We will
also elect to arrive there in the year 1862 A.D.
At the edge of that moss (take care of your feet,
please, it is rather treacherous ground) lies a boat.
Through all the years you have passed over—nearly
two thousand, remember—it has slept peacefully at
the bottom, comfortably happed up with the mud of
centuries; but it has been awakened and brought to

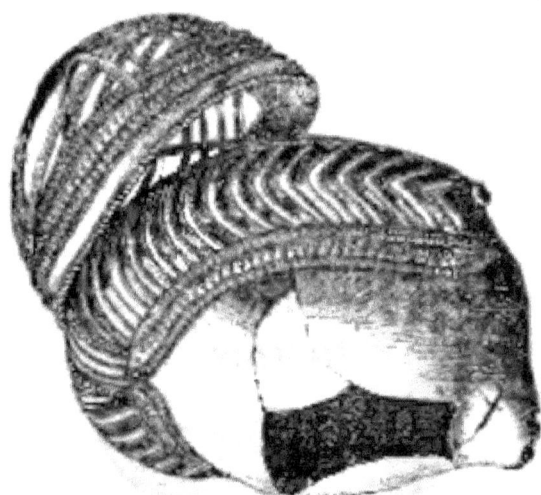

Richly-gilt silver Helmet, of Iron Age.

light to-day for your inspection. Look at it reverently,
youths and maidens, for it is older than the oldest
thing you can think of, yet it throbs with life and is
pregnant with human interest. It points with unerr-
ing finger, through all the intervening cycles, to the
time when the axe of the woodman cut and trimmed
these clean oaken ribs which have been painted black
enough since then, and to the day when the sure stroke
of the prehistoric hammer drove home the last clinker
which fastened the whole together, and sent the

F

finished vessel into its native element. It has besides
a thousand voices which tell of the manners and
customs, the condition and manufactures, of a people
hidden from us by a veil
so thickly woven by Time's
busy fingers, that it would
be, without such assist-
ance, all but impenetrable.
Fifty pairs of oars have
been used to propel this
ancient bark. It is built
of overlapping oak boards,

Gold Ring, set with precious
stones.

firmly held together by
iron rivets. A series of
projections have been left
on the inside of each
board during the cutting
process, and these have
each two little holes
pierced in them, through
which pass the ropes that

Gold Brooch, richly Jewelled.

fasten the sides of the vessel to the ribs. Now for
the freight. You may expect this to be no light
one in a vessel measuring seventy-five feet long,

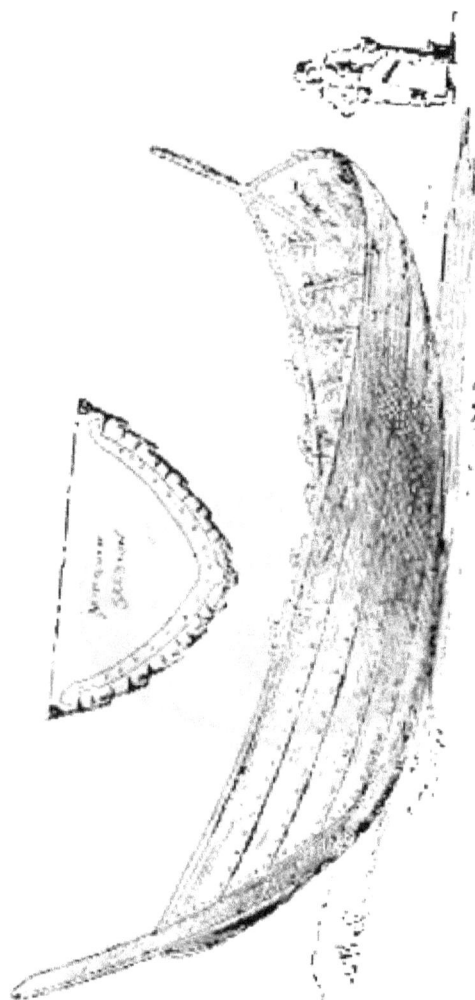

Prehistorio Boot Jound at Kyrksau (Norrkoping.)

Fig. 1

nine feet wide, and three feet deep. Numerous iron axes, swords, and lances are stowed away in one end, but the boat has been tilted over somewhat, and the rest of this interesting armoury is deposited among the poat. There you will see helmets, arrows, breast-plates, nearly a hundred swords, 500 spears, quantities of horse gear, and even coats of mail. But there are other objects here which tell us that the men of iron were occupied with something more than military manœuvres. In the bottom of that old boat of theirs there are some excellent spindle wheels, whet-stones, wooden rakes and mallets, a whole treasury of

Primitive threshing machine.—A modern instance of the use of flint. (From Syria.)

bronze brooches, and last of all, O ye housewives, two very superior birch brooms!

What a picture this heterogeneous collection brings before us of the tastes and habits, the homes and occupations of the men and women whose children we are. The origin of the Aryan seems as much a problem as ever, but we, like children, love to gather the little fragments of our unwritten history together, and with them try to form a mosaic which shall give us a clearer view and a fuller knowledge of the races that have lived before us. Here is scope enough for the wildest flights of fancy. You need not, however, be disappointed, if you find in our patchwork a section here which is upside down, and another there that does not match very well, for they are **hard to read** and harder still to **fit** together.

But we may not linger over a forgotten people and an obsolete age. Newer and wider fields appear as the first page of History opens before us; the cobwebs of conjecture and speculation are swept away by the chronicler's remorseless **hand**; slowly but surely the dawn creeps over the horizon of time, and the light of **truth** breaks **on a** world hitherto lost in fog, or illumined only by the treacherous will-o'-the-wisps **of** imagination and **surmise.**

CHAPTER IV.

THE LAND OF THE LOTUS.

Far down on the opposite side of the street live the people who come next on our visiting list. It is only just daybreak on the western side, up which we have been walking; but the sun rises in the east, so it has been daylight for ever so long over the way, and the people have done marvellous work since dawn. Cross over now, please, and make their acquaintance. It is just as well we did not go earlier, for though the sun has long been awake, the morning mists are only now rising to reveal the full beauty of this Eastern Wonderland. One by one the old cloud-curtains are gathered up and folded away for ever. One by one, out of darkness into daylight, steal those giant forms, men and structures, which must ever remain the delight and marvel of succeeding ages, until time shall be no more. As you approach them, look well at the people whose childhood is mythical—whose genius is inscrutable as their sphinxes. Whence they come, who they are, no man can say. As for their land, its rocks are bare, its plains monotonous; it is in form a lily, but a lily with a crooked stem, and you look in vain for charm of colour, for alternating sun and rain, or for any variety whatsoever. Yet does it hold men as by a spell; all are eager to read the story writ upon a thousand tombs, for the lotus blooms exhale a rare and mystic fragrance which none may resist.

Right through the land a river creeps: the beneficent author of all fertility in a desert of sand. This also is a mystery, and the people call it Hapi,

The Island of the Fiddle.

Amen-Ra. (From a bronze in the Louvre.) Height 22·04 inches.

"The Hidden," and Osiris, "The Good Being," and it is to them a god. Egypt, their very country itself, is the gift of this river-god, which you and I call Nile; and they say that he who has once tasted its sacred waters must evermore return to drink. Year by year they have seen it rise victorious over the desert, and they have reaped their harvests and found bread enough and to spare for their hungry ones. Do you wonder, then, that the Nile is above all gods save Ra, the Eternal Sun, the breath of whose nostrils gives life to the seed cast with faithful heart into the lap of the "Hidden" one?

It is but the beginning of the day, the dawn of history: 4000 years before the flight thither of the Holy Family of Nazareth, and we stand upon the very fringe of the great forest of the Unrevealed;

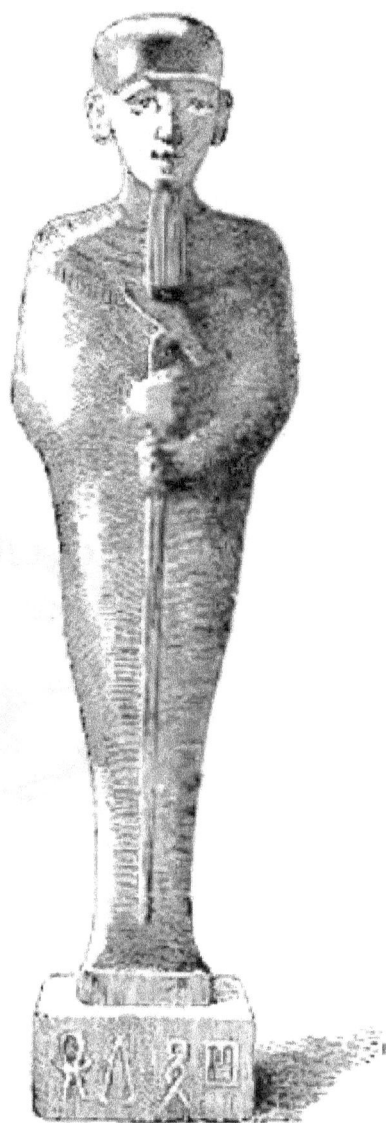

Ptah. (From a bronze in the Louvre.) Actual size.

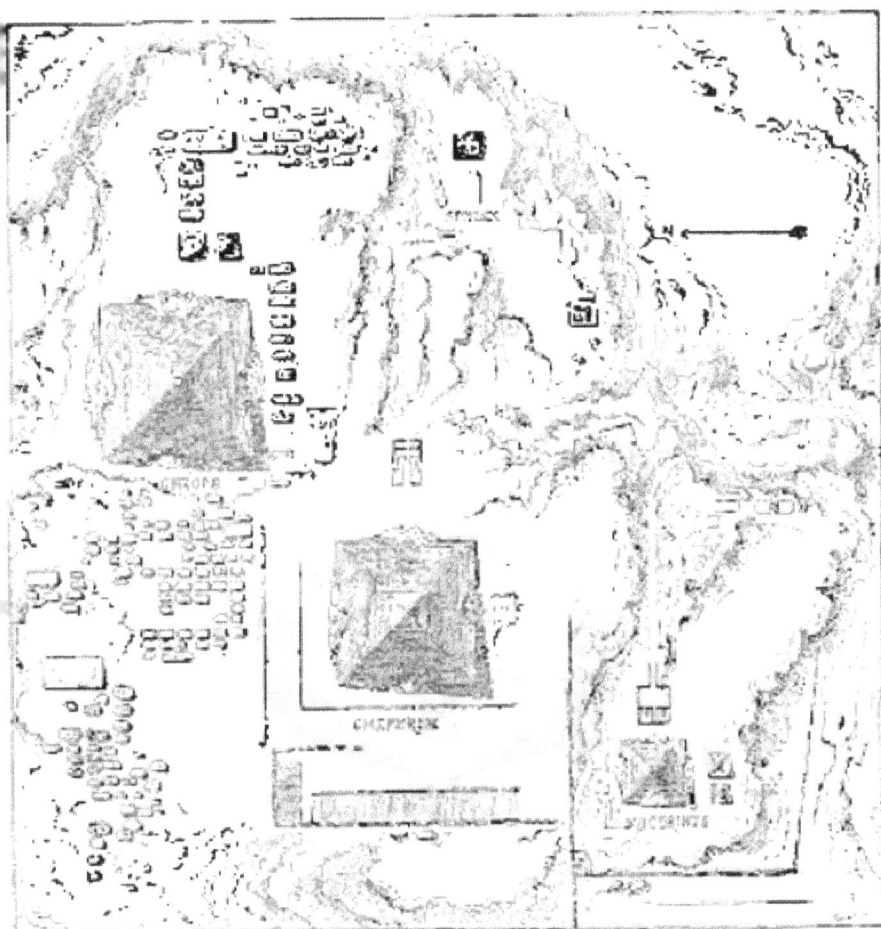

Plan of the Pyramids of Gizeh, and of that part of the necropolis which immediately surrounds them.

yet behold! out of the shadows comes a king—Menes by name—whose achievements bewilder us with their magnitude. No budding architect this, who defies Nature and turns the mighty Nile from its bed, that he may build his capital on the site he has chosen. The childhood of Menes and his people is beyond our ken ;

Sepulchral chamber of an Apis bull. (From Mariette.)

they burst upon us in the full rigour of maturity, and in all the glory of their marvellous genius. Their new city is called Memphis. It is the home of Ptah, the primeval god ; and the king has built here a wondrous temple, whose shrine, nine cubits high and eight cubits long, is approached by avenues of carven lions terrible to look upon.

But these venerable folk are firm believers in a future life; they call their houses "Hotels," their tombs "Eternal dwelling places," and they are even more careful in their provision for the dead than for the living. Here is their cemetery, the vastest in the world, stretching for twenty miles on either hand. We cannot traverse its myriad streets, so must be content to glance at the grandest of its monuments. There are the royal tombs, all pyramids; and deep in the sand on every side sleep their silent subjects. Here also is the tomb of the Apis Bull; a vast excavation, in whose many chambers are laid the mummified bodies of the sacred animals, each in a sarcophagus cut from one ponderous granite block weighing little short of seventy tons; and the cost of whose preparation, and accompaniments of jewels, statuettes and vases you may translate into your

The goddess Bast. (From a bronze in the Louvre.) Actual size.

own tongue as 20,000*l.*
Egypt is a land of gods
and "Hapi," the Apis
Bull is but a personifi-
cation of one of them—
Ptah, the everlasting.
I have already shown
you his portrait in the
character of the benefi-
cent creator, and beside
him stands Ra, the
great sun-god himself.
But here is another
pair of Nile deities,
Bast, that popular old
cat-goddess; and Thoth,
the essence of all wis-
dom and recorder of
weights. Besides these
you must see fair Isis
—some other time I will
tell you why she has a
cow's head—and the
terrible and malignant
Touaris, with hippo-
potamus' head and cro-
codile's back. In spite
of all these gods and a
hundred others I might
show you, there are
many thoughtful minds
in the Lotus Land that
acknowledge but one
supreme being. The
upper ten, however,
kings and nobles, de-
light in endowing each

Thoth. (Louvre.) Enamelled
clay. Actual size.

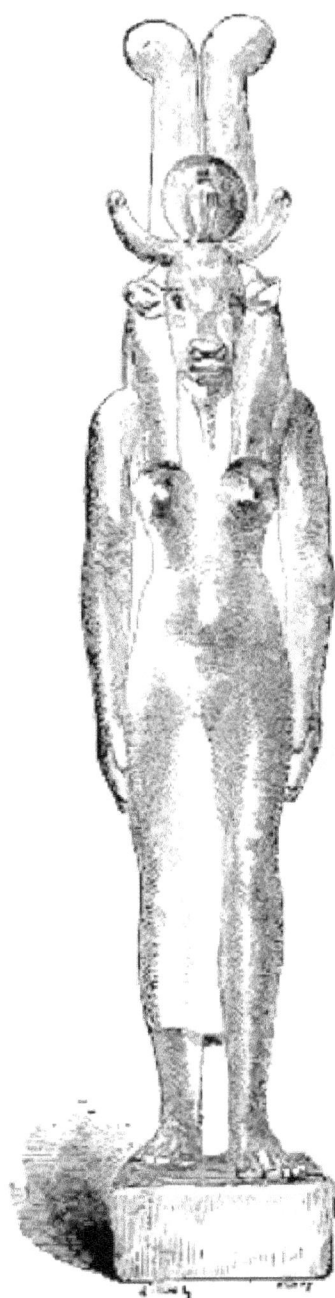

attribute of the deity with separate existence; while the common people do not even reach this altitude, but worship what they can see—the hawk, ibis, and bull, equally with the leek and the onion, so that it becomes a reproach that the Egyptians do not disdain to worship gods which grow in their own gardens. In the northern house of the iron men, the Sun was the centre of all adoration; here you see it is still the sun that heads the pantheon. You must look at these two scarabs, both sun ships; and strangely like those of prehistoric times. One shows the sun-disc supported by snakes, while the other has the birds at stem and stern which signify motion, as in the age of Iron. Many of the old sacred symbols, the snake spiral, the zigzag, etc., have become mere designs in decoration, however, and the ideas of divinity have taken more definite shape since we left the men of metal behind.

As we pass along, Menes, the hoary, disappears. Six royal dynasties reign in Memphis; then a cloud gathers once more over the land, and is not once lifted for many centuries. I will only stop to introduce to

Isis-Hathor. (Louvre.) Bronze. Actual size.

you four out of the long lines of kings who make up
these dynasties. They are of the fourth royal line, and
their names are Seneferu, Khufu, Khafra, and Menkaura.
These are, above all, the pyramid builders of Egypt.

Seneferu is the founder of his
house and the conqueror of
the land of Sinai. Khufu, or
Cheops, as you may prefer to
call him, is his son; Khafra
or Chephren is his near de-
scendant; and Menkaura is
Chephren's son. Khufu and
Khafra are hard men and
cruel, but Menkaura is mer-
ciful and beloved of the
people. His father's deeds
are displeasing to him, "he
both opened the temples and
gave liberty to the people
who were ground down to
the last extremity, to return
to their own business and to
their sacrifices. Also he
gave decisions of their causes,
juster than those of all the
other kings."[1] If you come
with me some day to the
great treasure-house of the
richest city in the modern
world, I will show you the
bones of this good Menkaura.

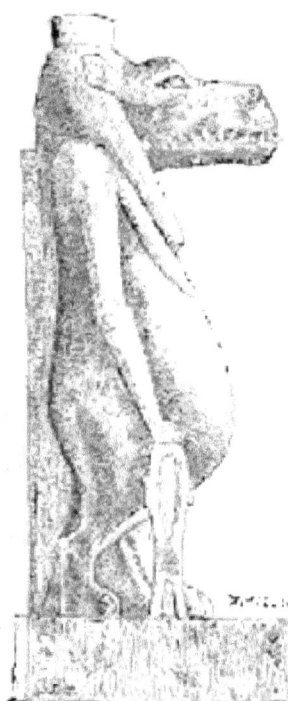

Touaris. Boolak. (Drawn
by G. Bénédite.)

After forty centuries' repose among the lilies of Egypt,
he has been carried to his last resting-place at your
very door.

The pyramid of Seneferu, though not the largest, is
the oldest in the world. Nearly 6000 years have gone

[1] Herodotus.

Statue of Chephren.   Height five feet seven inches.   (Bulak)
Drawn by G. Bénédite.

by since its first stone was laid. Yonder rise the two
built by Chephren and Menkaura; to the north stands
the great pyramid, Khufu's work 5000 years ago.
Look at it and marvel: 480 feet is the height of it, and
764 feet the length of each side; it covers more than
thirteen acres, and its cubic contents would build a
city of 22,000 ordinary houses. Nearly seven million
tons is the weight of it, and 100,000 men laboured for
twenty years to complete it. What would we not give
to know *how* they moved those stupendous granite
blocks into place? Here are some basement stones
thirty feet long, five feet high, and as many wide.
Imagination fails when we try to understand how these
men handled objects of such colossal proportions; yet
there they are before you—the most amazing of all
human constructions, adamantine in their strength,
and as the everlasting hills in their duration.

But I did not bring you out this morning to stupefy
you with superlatives! Leave now this city of the
dead, and come with me to Thebes. Here everything
pulsates with life. Close by the river's brink stands
Luxor; further off you see Karnak, the Rameseum and
Medeenet-Aboo. The city is called Nu-Amen, "The
city of Amen-ra," for Amen is the god of it. They also
call it Ta-Apiu or Thebes, "The City of Thrones."

Gorgeous palaces, still more gorgeous temples, monuments, and obelisks continue to proclaim the glory of
the Lily-Land; but there is a human interest here, for
which we looked in vain at Memphis. Thebes is
covered within and without with pictures of men and
gods, and they tell the story of many a dynasty—many
a change. You may read of the victories of Shishak,
and how Pharaoh, the oppressor, made a treaty with
that remarkable people, the Hittites.

Where can you match the marvellous columns in the
temple of Amen at Karnak? Those in the centre are
the loftiest ever reared by hand of men in any edifice;

o

Entrance to the Hypostyle Hall of the Temple of Amen, at Karnak.

109 feet from floor to ceiling! Two monarchs have spent their lives in constructing them, and now the son of the last of these devotes all the time he can spare from his many campaigns, in putting the finishing touches to a monument worthy alike of its royal builders and its more than royal inmate. Here are the portraits of those temple builders, Pharaohs both of them, Seti and his son Rameses II. I daresay you are a trifle confused among the many Pharaohs of the Lily-Land. The name is a sacred one, and should really be rendered " Phrah," for, being interpreted, it means the Sun. In Thebes itself, the Sun is called " Piré ;" but in Memphis, the more classic city, it is " Phré," and pronounced " Phra," and from being used to signify a worshipper and child of the great divinity, the name has become the distinctive title of long dynasties of Egyptian kings. This Pharaoh, Rameses II., should interest you more than all the rest. He is not only the constructor, with his father Seti, of those matchless pillars, but he is the oppressor of the Children of Israel ; the tyrant who says they shall build up his treasure-cities of Pithom and Raouses, yet laughs when they ask for straw to make the bricks thereof. His fair young daughter, Nefer-t-ari, has taken the little Moses from his nest of rushes by the river side ; she tenderly cherishes the child and educates him in all the wisdom, art, and science of her country ; but her father does not trouble his head about this mad fancy for a Hebrew lad ; his time and attention are far too much occupied in affairs relating to his own aggrandizement.

Oh yes! he is a great king and—to the lotus-folk— a very god is this Rameses. Stones turn to gold at his touch : his enemies flee before him and his lion : he is proud, but not too proud to strike the names off the pillars which record the brave deeds of dead Pharaohs and to inscribe his own in the vacant places.

If we did not know his tricks, you and I, we might give him the credit of the great and good actions of a score of kings—which is exactly what he intends.   He

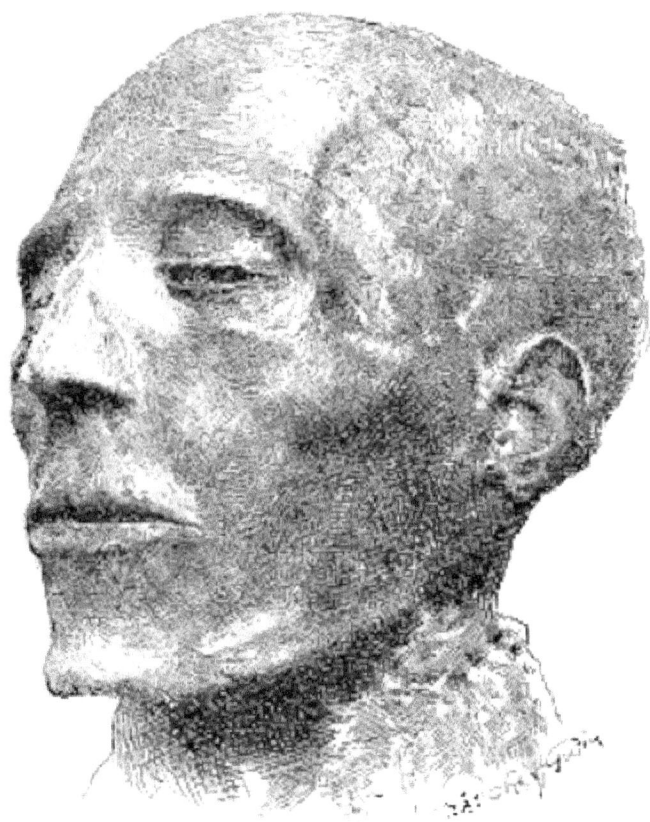

A Mummy's Head: the King Seti I.   (From a photograph taken from the corpse, preserved in the Museum at Boulak.)

has a charmed life, and all but reaches the perfect span of 110 years, which every good Egyptian prays for ; but the pale horseman does overtake him at last, and

he is carried to his glorious sepulchre by a weeping
and disconsolate nation. After lying there for 3000
years, he has been taken from his mummy shroud,
and this is a true portrait of the Pharoah of the
oppression, as he is to-day.

There is another Pharaoh, one Khuenaten, with
whom I must make you acquainted. He is of an older
dynasty than Rameses II., and should have been pre-

Rameses II. in his chariot: the King's Son charges by the
side of the horses.

sented to you before the latter, for more reasons than
one. His is the great Renaissance period in Egyptian
art. Nowhere else you will see such fine realistic treatment of objects as is carried on here. In the animals
painted on the floor of the palace harem, you have the
very earliest known examples of foreshortening and the
portrayal of rapid action. Before we leave our lotus
friends behind, however, we shall have to visit the art
school of this enlightened king. But Khuenaten is

more than an artist; he is a re-
former of religion and ethics. From
his mother, Queen Tii, of Mesopotamia, he learned that there is but
one god, and he has no respect for
the polytheistic doctrines of his
subjects: so he has built him a
new city, Khuenaten the "City of
Aten," or the Sun-disc, for this is
the sole deity he acknowledges, and
he has discarded his original name
of Amenophis and taken that of his
city and of his god. The court is
removed from Thebes to the city
where Aten alone is god, and the
name of Amen is blotted out from
every monument in the land. The
people don't take to this new heresy
at all kindly, but Khuenaten keeps
them in good humour by presents
of bracelets and golden collars,
which are distributed wholesale on
high days and holidays. Everybody is satisfied with this little
concession except the scribes: they
are not at all pleased to have so
much extra work imposed on them;
for all gifts have to be registered,
as well as the names of those who
receive them. The religion of the
disc-worshippers, if not quite perfect, is higher and purer than its
predecessors, and while Khuenaten
lives things go smoothly enough,
but in a few generations there
arises a king who loves not the
sun-disc: the old religion is

The names of
Ramases II.

restored and the heresy of Aten stamped out of
Egypt.

Just one other monarch I want you to know—a

Rameses II.   (From a photograph of the corpse, preserved in the
Boulak Museum.)

lady this time—Queen Hatasu by name. Hatasu is a
usurper, her brother, Thothmes III., being their
father's legal successor; but Thothmes is young, and

his sister quite objects to play second fiddle; so, for
seventeen years, she has reigned over Egypt, much to
the advantage of all concerned.   They call her the
"Man-queen," and she is in no way offended, for to be
considered a man, or equal to a man, is Hatasu's dearest ambition.   Like many other people with hobbies,
she overrides hers, however; wears an artificial beard,
and calls herself the king.   Her inscriptions get
terribly mixed up sometimes, and such sentences as

Painted Floor of Khuenaten's Harem.

"his majesty herself" are of frequent occurrence.
Notwithstanding these little foibles, Hatasu is one of
the most intelligent and far-seeing rulers the Children
of the Nile have ever had.   She has built ships—the
first that ever sailed on the Red Sea—and sent an
expedition to the land of Punt, which is Arabia, and
has established free trade between Egypt and that land
of spices.   The people of Punt are pile-dwellers, and
they have a dwarf queen, who gladly consents to let
Hatasu enter her groves and dig up trees to transplant

to the far-off Lotus-Land; precious gums, too, she gathers in sacks, and they float down the Nile on the

The King (Amenophis IV.) and his Family throwing Golden Collars to the People.

decks of the new ships, protected from the sun by huge awnings. The dwarf-queen returns with the party to Egypt, and Hatasu makes a grand festival to celebrate

the event. She also builds a temple to Ammon near
Thebes, and causes the doings of her merchant fleet to
be engraved on the walls. Her gold-crowned obelisk
at Karnak is the loftiest that you will find entire in the

People adoring the giver of the Collars.

world, and her brother Thothmes, who solves the succession difficulty by first collaborating with, and finally
displacing Hatasu, has built one with which you are
very familiar. It is called Cleopatra's Needle, but it is

The Scribe registering the Golden Collars.

inscribed with the name of Thothmes III., brother of
the man-queen Hatasu.

So much for kings and queens; but you can have a
closer peep at the home-life of those old Egyptians if
you like. Very good; nothing could please me better,

and if you will just hurry up a little, we will overtake that merry throng, and see whence they are bound, and what they have to say for themselves. A dinner-party! Well, we are in luck, for, to tell the truth, I was beginning to feel that a little refreshment would not come amiss after our morning's meander in this rather dry district. Have no anxiety about your coat; the *barber* is a much more important individual here than the tailor, for every man's head must be shaved, and there is no more emphatic way of depicting a person of low habits than by giving him a beard.

Here we are at our destination, and in plenty of time,

1. Stone Scarabæus from Cyprus.   2. Stone Scarabæus (Sun-ships, with birds at the prow).

too, so you may spend a minute in examining the exterior of our host's mansion, before passing inside with the rest of the guests. We are evidently about to be entertained by a gentleman of some standing, for this is decidedly above the average run of Egyptian habitations. The houses of the common folk are more like that uninviting-looking structure in the rear. It is quite a mistake to imagine that these people are a melancholy race. The fact is, you will find them rather hilarious this afternoon; still, there is no denying it, they spend a considerable portion of their life in preparing to die, and they are usually quite content with a temporary house of sun-dried bricks to live in, whilst their tombs, whatever else they are, are certainly made to last. As I remarked before, this is an exceptionally fine specimen of a private dwelling, and the builders of

From Cleopatra's Needle (B.C. 1450).

it are architects whom you will find it hard to beat even at the top of our street. What could be more graceful than those tall, slender, lily-stem columns crowned with their capitals of lotus flowers? Can you

The Barber and his Customer.

imagine anything prettier than that overhanging cornice, which is quite a feature in Egyptian architecture? I dare say it strikes you that the lighting arrangements might be improved. Wait till you are inside, my friend. You have an Eastern climate to deal with here, and sulphurous fogs are not an every-day occurrence, so there is not the same objection to an open roof that exists in some localities you may have read of. These Egyptians

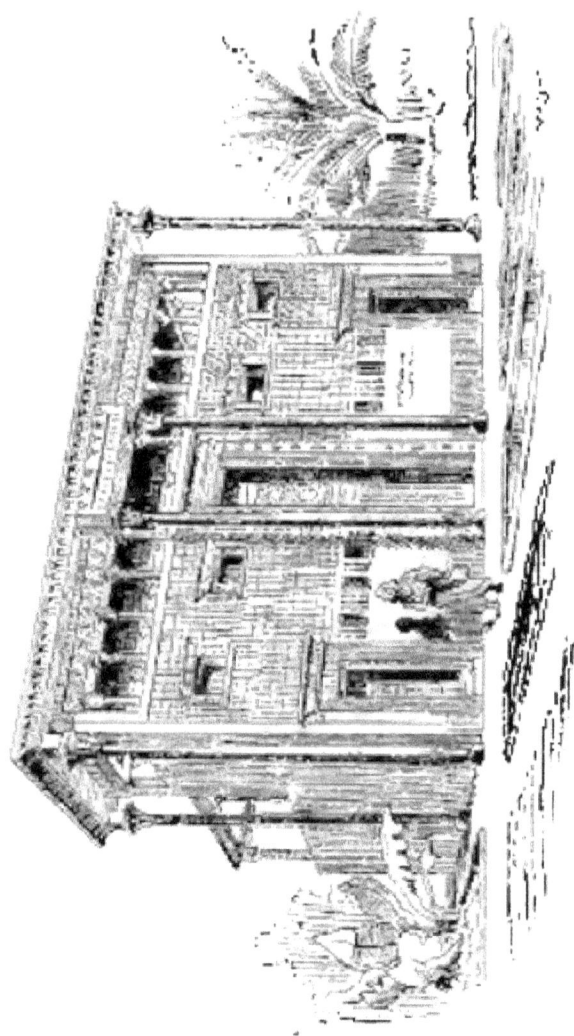

Egyptian Mansion.

prefer their rooms top-lit, let me tell you, and a very
good idea too. The courts and windows of the best
houses are supported on columns, and the porch—also
of columns—has a lintel bearing the name of the owner.

But I don't fancy cold goose—and the Egyptians,
sensible people, dine at noon—so let us look in and
see how things are progressing. Ah! the host has
been called away for half an hour, hence there is a little
delay about the dinner, and we shall just have time
to walk through the kitchen and inspect the cooking.

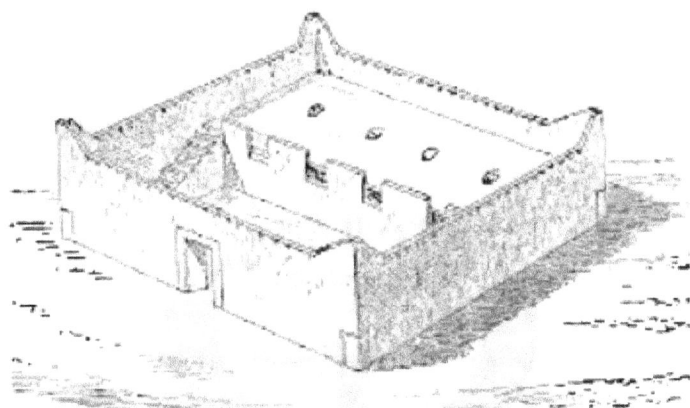

Model of an Egyptian house.   (Louvre.)

The cauldrons on the dresser are well filled (those birds
look anything but comfortable, and every moment I
expect to see them step out on to the table); beef, fish,
game, vegetables, and, I do declare, here are some first-
rate black puddings. Plenty of bread and cakes with
carraway seeds, and—yes—I *thought* I smelt goose!
There they are, frizzling over the charcoal fire, whilst
the legs of lamb simmer quietly in the broth-pot. You
are quite astonished at the domestic arrangements, and
well you may be, for the inscriptions on the wall tell
you—if you can read them—that you are walking

On the kitchen dresser is an ample store of viands. The scullion plucks the goose for the cook to roast, while into the pot go the joints, which are stowed later on. And the butler carves the meal ready for table.

In the meantime the sweeper is ready with his palm-fibre broom, and the steward comes with an inkhorn to see the cleaning up. The cook rushes in hot and vigous with the dishes, while the house servant sprinkles the floor for the comfort of the guests. And now the hasty messenger informs the burly porter that the master is coming home in his chariot.

through a kitchen which was furnished a thousand years before ever Moses made his appearance in the land of the lotus. Now for the dining-room and dinner, if you please. There is no end of a commotion here. The steward is not at all satisfied with the way the floor has been swept, and the housemaid has totally forgotten till this minute to water it. Amid considerable excitement, in rushes the cook with the dishes, for the porter has just been informed that the master is coming. Here is your seat (a whole one if you are single; married people only get one between them), and a couple of servants to anoint your head, wash your hands, and give you a general brush-up. And there come the host and his wife at last. They take their places at the end of the room on a sort of double chair, and the feast begins. As dinner proceeds, you are entertained with music and a variety of skilful athletics. The Egyptians are skilful gymnasts, but, be it known, they leave boxing severely alone. It may be a desirable accomplishment, but the gentlemanly Egyptian of 4000 years ago does not appear to think so, and I am not sure that I don't agree with him. He spends his time more profitably in other pursuits—shoe-making, glass-blowing, meat-curing, etc., as you will gather from these rows of workers outside. He is likewise a skilful metallurgist, but his patience and accurate working are best shown in his cabinet-making, the veneering, glueing, and dovetailing of which are truly marvellous. No one knows so well as he the art of mural decoration, and, as an architect, he is as much at home in light and delicate structures as in those everlasting monuments which have never, and can never be surpassed. Nothing comes amiss to him: he is the inventor of the arch as well as of artificial egg-hatching, and already he divides his year into twelve months of thirty days each, and uses a decimal and duodecimal system of calculation. He is, above

During the repast the guests are amused by harp and pipe; and further entertained by display of skill at tumbling, wrestling, and singlestick.

EGYPTIAN HANDICRAFT AND RECREATION.

The scribe with sheets and palette. The cabinet-maker with his bow-drill. The goldsmith with his blowpipe. The ... and others brandishing a mirror.

B

all, a model husband and father, spending many a spare
hour in constructing those fearful and wonderful toys
you see in the hands of his little girls, wooden dolls

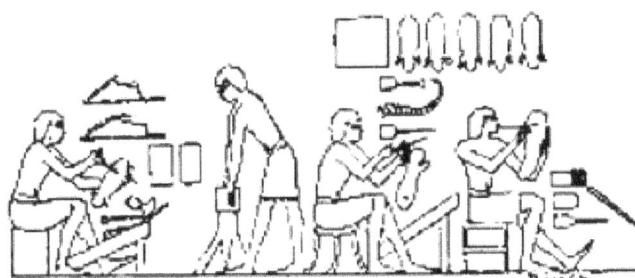

A Shoemaker's Workshop.

with strings of beads for hair, cats with movable jaws,
and creatures of a nondescript character, with jointed
limbs, all just as delightful to the Egyptian nurslings

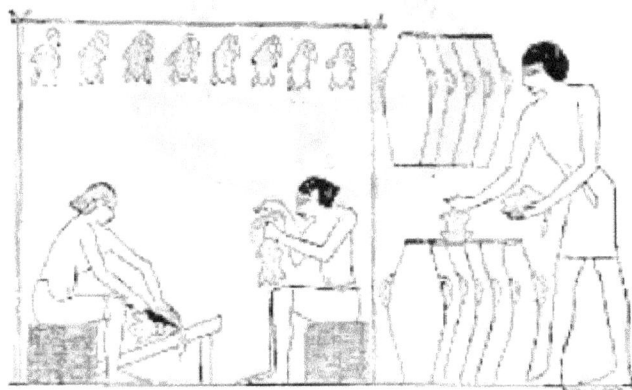

Preserving Game in salt.

as your own fine mechanical toys to children you may
have a rather closer interest in.

Idleness and insubordination are not, however, per-

mitted in man or beast. The very cats are trained as
retrievers, and the monkeys gather the fruit, whilst the
crocodiles step nimbly out of the water when called by
name, and cheerfully submit to have their ears pierced
merely that you may see how they look with earrings!

Now let me prevail upon you to taste this beer.
It is the Egyptian Allsopp's very best—made of red

Fowling with cats upon the Pond.

barley and bittered with lupins. I don't believe they
know anything about hops. They are terrible beer-
drinkers here, I am sorry to say, and even go so far as
to express, on their sepulchral tablets, the hope that
they may have jugs of beer in the other world. Stimu-
lants are used to excite the palate before drinking;
cabbages, for instance, are in great demand. I fail to
see the stimulating properties of this excellent viand
myself; with me it has frequently had rather a de-

pressing influence, but certain it is the thirsty
Egyptian finds it answer his purpose.

The teetotallers superciliously sniff at their lotus

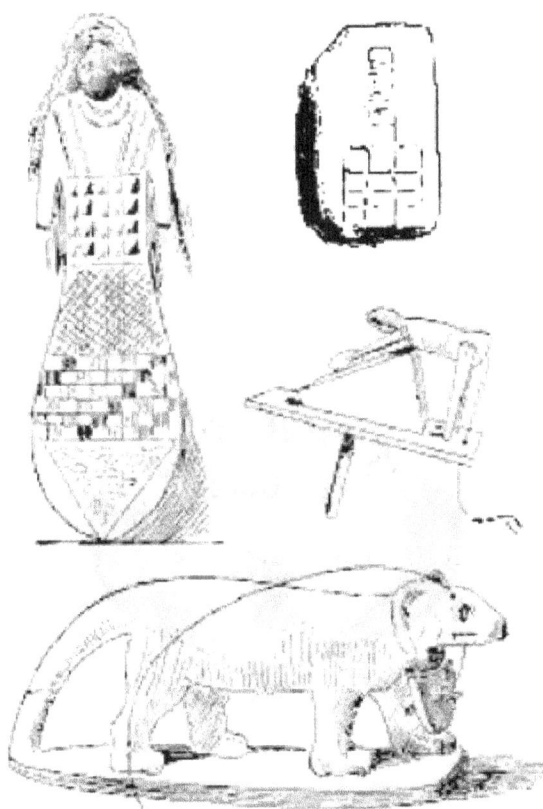

Egyptian Toys of 3000 years ago.

flowers and decline to notice the bottle, no offence
being taken thereat. The wine, however, is circulating
freely, and the guests are pretty lively. The host is
deep in a game of chess, and in spite of the mummy,

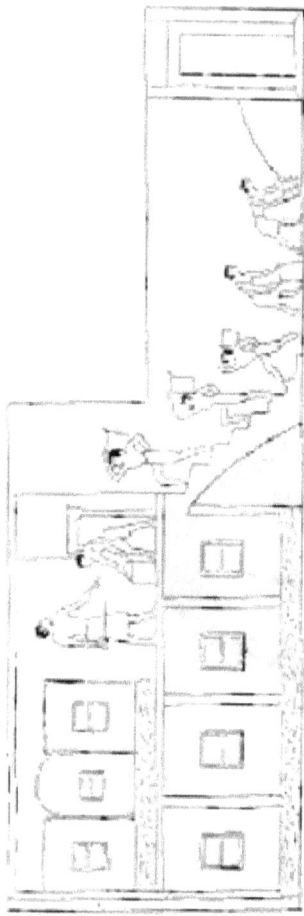

Baumbg. Egat Karmo. (From Champollion, pl. 396.)

The Egyptian bakery. The dough is kneaded in the big looking bowl and carried in a jar to the baking table. Close by stands the hearth where the cakes are baked, and the baker's man waits to carry them off on his tray when finished.

which the priests think proper to drag round the
room as a gentle hint of the transitoriness of most
earthly pleasures, the atmosphere is anything but de-
pressing. As the conversation becomes animated the
ladies take to criticizing each other's clothes, and, I
regret to say, can't hold their tongues even about the
furniture and plate of their host. Quantity, quality,
and prices of the viands are freely discussed, and the
host is expected to be highly gratified at the comments
made. In the midst of all this chatter, one of those

Scool : inlaid Ivory and Ebony.

harmless but very awkward young men we all know so
well, leans too heavily against some temporary decora-
tions, and down comes the whole paraphernalia—youth
and all, on the astonished gossipers. What confusion,
screams, and uplifting of hands to protect the nicely-
oiled wigs! but nobody is hurt; the youth is dismissed
with an admonition, and the ladies flutter down to their
chat again.

I am sorry to hurry you, but if you have finished
your dinner, I would like a word with the undertakers

at the back door. The mummy they are bandaging with those gummed linen bands is nearly completed,

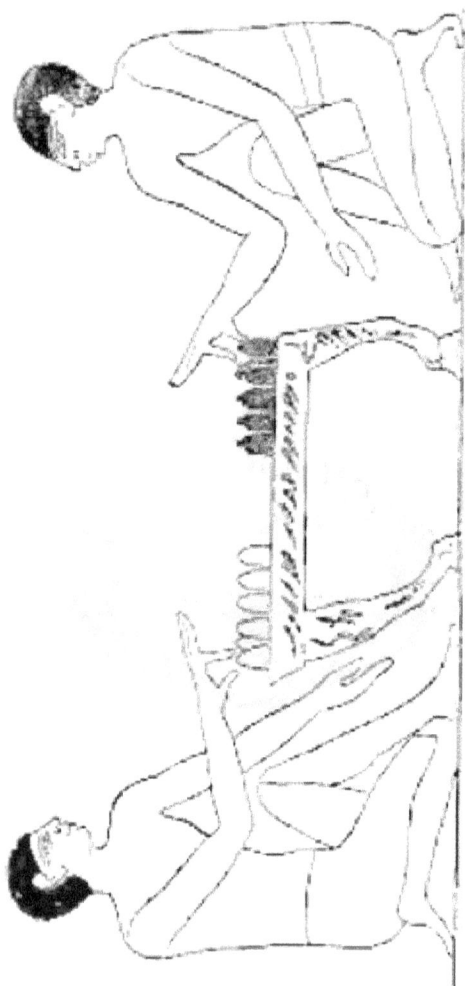

Chess-players, Beni Hassan.   (Champollion, pl. 388.)

and it has been about ten weeks in preparation, they tell me. The brain has been extracted through the nose with a hook, and the intestines drawn from the body through an incision in the side. After much cleansing, the cavities were filled with spices and sewn up. Then it lay in salt for seventy days, and is now receiving the finishing touches before being given back to the relatives, who will fasten it into an ornamental case and set it upright in a room in the house. It has cost 250*l*.; but there is another and cheaper method where no incision is required. Cedar oil is injected by means of syringes, and the body salted as before. The cedar oil is strong enough to bring away the intestines in a state of dissolution, and as the salt dissolves the flesh, nothing is left but skin and bone. This costs 80*l*., but the poorest classes cannot afford even that amount, and have to be satisfied with the seventy days' salting.

These curious figures of glazed ware are "Ushabti," or "Answerers," and they are placed in the tombs that they may do the work of the dead in the other world. A great advance this, over the practice of using human victims for such an office, and saying much for the humanity and civilization of these ancient Egyptians, don't you think?

It is not every one who is allowed the privilege of keeping his deceased relations at home. The benefits of having them so handily near are manifold. Besides a soul, "Ba," which temporarily leaves him at death, every man has a "Ka," or "double," which continues to exist and to represent the actual person after the latter ceases to live. It is necessary that the body should be preserved against any chance of decay in order that the soul may be able to inhabit it again in the future, so, in addition to the mummification process, there is a continual supply of food, etc., placed before the statue of the "Ka," all of which goes to sustain the departed. Indeed, the tombs and their inhabitants but repeat in shadow the dwellings and

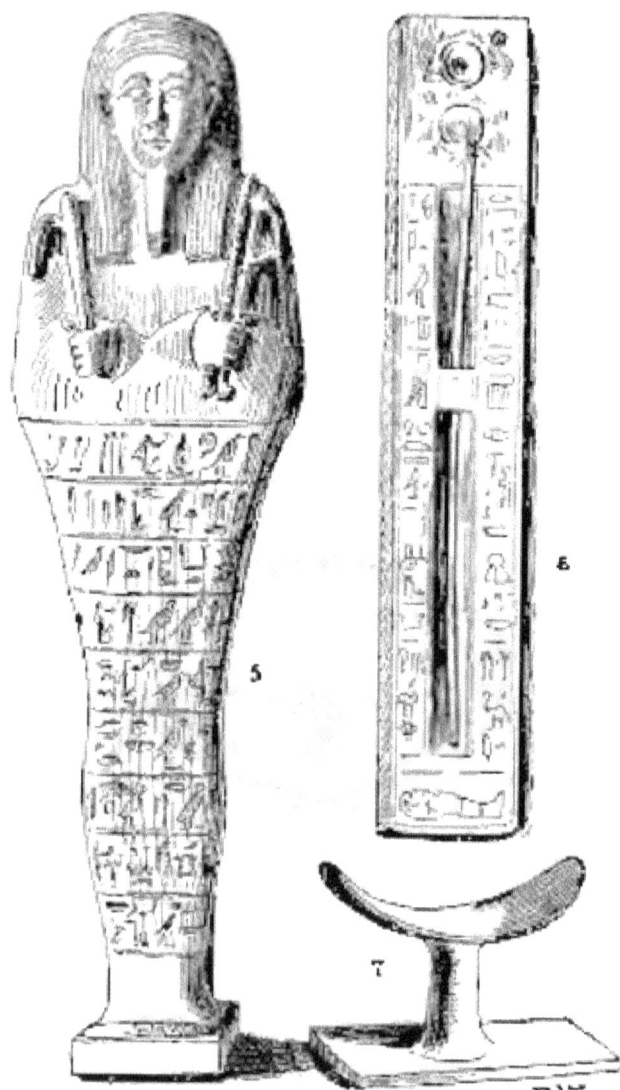

5. Ushabti, or sepulchral figure inscribed with the 6th chapter of
the Book of the Dead; age about 2600 years (from a fine example in the possession of the writer) (⅓). 6. Wooden palette
with reed brush and depressions for colour (⅔). 7. Head-
rest for the dead (⅓).

every-day life of the people, and woe betide the unlucky
householder who neglects to keep the "doubles" of his
departed ones in every comfort. Hence the advantage
of having no long journey to take when paying his
periodical visits to the "Ka." Generally, however, the
body is placed in a tomb, high above the Nile's reach,
and every care taken to conceal the entrance. The
tomb is the very earliest
architectural edifice: the
pyramid is the legitimate
and more enduring successor
of the tumulus. In the
land of the lotus, ready-
made tombs are kept in
stock, inscribed with the
usual invocations, blanks
being left for the name
and biography of the future
purchaser and occupier.
They vary in form; but
suppose you look into this
one! It is the type known
as Mastaba, and contains
three distinct chambers.
The first we enter is above
ground and has no door.
The walls are covered with
pictures, many of them
highly comic; you are surprised to see Egyptian

Upper chamber, well, and
mummy chamber of Mastaba.

humour is irrepressible! That upright stone at
one side facing east, is an indispensable adjunct;
it is the stele, and is inscribed with all the
virtues of the deceased; near it stands the table for
offerings—the only piece of furniture in the place.
This is the reception room of the "Ka," open to all
and sundry, and just beyond is a corridor nearly

Stele of Nefer-aun. (Boulak.)

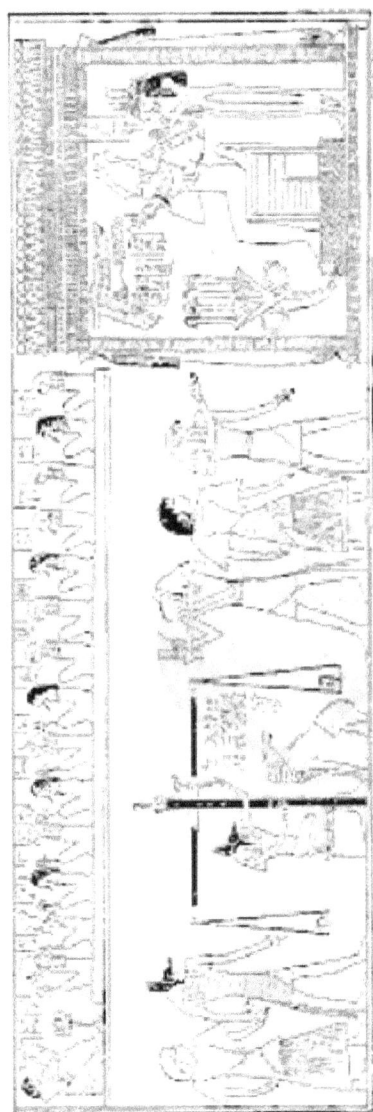

The Judgment of the Soul at the Tribunal of Osiris.

walled up, for the exclusive use of the statues of the dead. Finally here is the pit or well from forty to eighty feet deep, at the bottom of which lies the mummy in a huge granite sarcophagus weighing many tons. Everything is lowered down the shaft by ropes, and a difficult and dangerous business it is. Seti and Rameses adopted an easier plan, and their tombs are simply rock-cut chambers with no well. "After death comes the judgment;" so believed the ancient Egyptian, and here stands the soul of the departed between Truth and Justice, awaiting his doom or his reward. Osiris sits enthroned with the sacred balance be-

fore him, and Thoth records the sentence as the heart
and deeds of the culprit are weighed against truth
and rectitude.

A unique cemetery came to light the other day,
which you may as well know about. How astonished
the poor fellah must have been who, digging by chance
in the sand, struck—cats! Cats of all sorts and sizes,
hundreds and thousands of cats; miles of cats! It
was something to see, I can tell you, that ponderous
wall of cats that grew out of the thrown-up contents

Table for offerings.   (Louvre.)

of this unheard-of cemetery. Every baby got a
mummied cat to play with, the boys made footballs of
them, till somebody saw that money might be made
out of those ancient pussies, and they were carted off
to make manure, soap, glue, paint, or anything else
that the fertile imaginations of their purchasers might
devise.

But you are fidgeting to get away from this grue-
some corner, so we will just glance into the school hard
by, and that will do for this morning. Stone, leather
and linen are all used to write on, but papyrus is
always chosen for literary work, official documents, and

Sarcophagus of Khoo-foo-Ankh. Perspective of low foreground. Red granite. Height 1-33 metres. (Boulak.)

for the book of the dead. To prepare it, these boys
are cutting the interior of the stalks into thin longi-
tudinal slices. Laying these in rows on the table,
they place over them a second layer, but at right

The smaller sarcophagus chamber in the tomb of Rameses VI.
(From Horeau, pl. 21.)

angles, joining the surfaces together with glue. When
pressed and dried, this strip of papyrus will measure from
6 to 14 inches wide, and may either be 2 inches or 150
feet long. The scribe writes with a reed and carries
red and black colours in the hollows of his palette—

Battle of the Oxen and Rats.   (From Thebes.)

here is a wooden
one with five reeds
still in it. It
would take far too
long to explain
them all, but I
know you would
be interested to
understand some
of those beautiful
characters he is
so busily writing.
That last word is
" Kleopatra," and
each hieroglyph re-
presents both the
appearance and the
initial of a Coptic
word. Let us look
at them in turn.
That funny triangle
is a knee, and a
knee in Coptic
begins with "k:"
below it is a lion,
the Coptic of which
has the initial "l."
Next comes a reed,
beginning in Coptic
with "E" or "A";
a noose, "O": a
mat or rectangle,
"P": an eagle,
"A": a hand, "T":
a mouth, "r": and
another eagle, "A"
again. The last

two signs are extra ones, always placed after a woman's

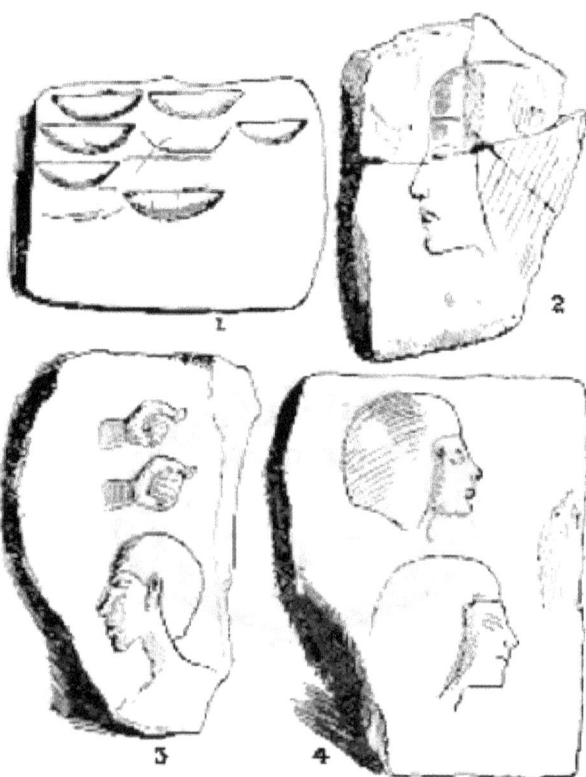

The sculptor's school of 3000 years ago.

1. The sign NEB as set for the students to copy. 2. Sculptor's trial piece: Queen Tii. 3, 4. Show master's work and students' copies.

name. The upper one is equivalent to "t"; the lower is an egg, signifying fertility. Plurality is expressed

I

by repeating signs: ⌡ is a seat: ⌡ ⌡ seats: ⌐ means a god; ⌐⌐⌐ gods: and many combinations are made. ⌐ is "a plough"; ⌐ "a mouth," and ⌐ "water"; but ⌐ means "beloved," and ⌐ "a name." Very often the object is placed after the word to make the

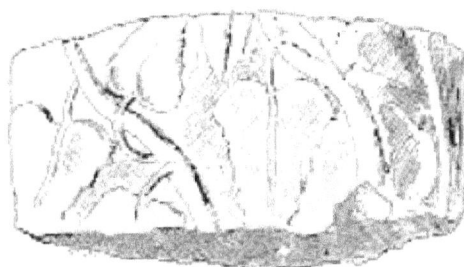

Khnenaten's art school.
1. Sculptured pillar. _ 2. The king adoring.   3. Khnenaten's death-mask.

meaning more clear: ⌐ ⌐ spells âpś, "a tortoise"; but this is how it is written ⌐ ⌐ 🐢

This papyrus contains the story of Isis. Shall we read it?

"Long, long ago, the gods reigned over men, yet they dwelt not upon the earth, but in the world that is

Egyptian art and industry of 3300 years ago.
8. Hard stone pivot for potters' wheel (?) 9. Wine jar ($\frac{1}{10}$).
10. Dish cover ($\frac{1}{5}$). 11. Painted vase ($\frac{1}{4}$). 12. Ditto ($\frac{1}{4}$).
13. Brick made by the Hebrews under Pharaoh, and bearing
his stamp ($\frac{1}{15}$). 14. Wooden sickle with flint teeth ($\frac{1}{4}$).

T 2

above the earth.   In process of time, however, they put
on the likeness of men and descended and ruled by
turns over the Lotus-Land.   And when it came to the
lot of Osiris, the son of Sab and Nut, he became a great
king and bountiful to the people.   Now his brother
Set hated him for the good he did, and for the love the
people bore him, so he slew Osiris and cast his body
into the Nile and it floated away to the sea.   But at
last the waves carried it to the Syrian shores, and there
it was found by Isis, sister and widow, who had sought it
with tears many days.   When Set heard this, he departed quickly and stole the body from Isis, and cut it
into fourteen pieces, and hid each piece in a secret place.
Then Isis made her a boat of papyrus, light and swift,
and sought again many more days for her lord, whom,
when she had found every part, she buried with great
honours.   Then Isis said to Horus her son, "Rise up, I
beseech thee, and seize thine uncle Set, and make his
life a burden to him, for this evil he hath done."
And Horus made war on Set and took him cap-
tive.   But when Isis beheld Set, who was also her
brother, in his dungeon, her heart waxed soft, and she
repented that she had caused him to be bound, and
she unloosed his bonds.   And Horus was wroth when
he heard it, and he came near to Isis, and took off her
crown and smote her, that her head came off.   And he
made war upon his uncle Set once more, and drove his
spear through Set's head and slew him.   But Thoth
had compassion on Isis and gave her a cow's head
instead of the head that Horus her son had struck
off."

So now you know the reason why Isis has a cow's
head instead of a woman's.

I would like to tell you about Thoth and his book,
and many other Nile stories quite as fascinating as that
of Isis.

I wish also we had time to examine the methods of

the students more closely, for you cannot but be struck
with the wonderful painting on their vases, and the
fidelity with which they copy the examples of head and
hand set by the
master. The pupil
draws the design in
red lines, which the
master corrects, and
the sculptor then
cuts away the stone
round the outlines,
leaving the design
in very low relief. A
coat of white is laid
on, and the painting
and varnishing com-
pletes the work.
Things are a little
dusty in the school,
for the workmen are
repairing the wall,
so come outside
again and look at
these bricks. They
are of unusual size,
but what will inter-
est you most is the
fact that they have
actually been made
by those unfortunate
Hebrews whose very
name is an abomina-
tion to Pharaoh.
You can see the
king's stamp on every one of them.

As we pass along the road, we hear the reapers
and the milkmaids singing in the fields on each side.

Ploughing: from the Necropolis of Memphis.

And now, before you go, I must tell you something

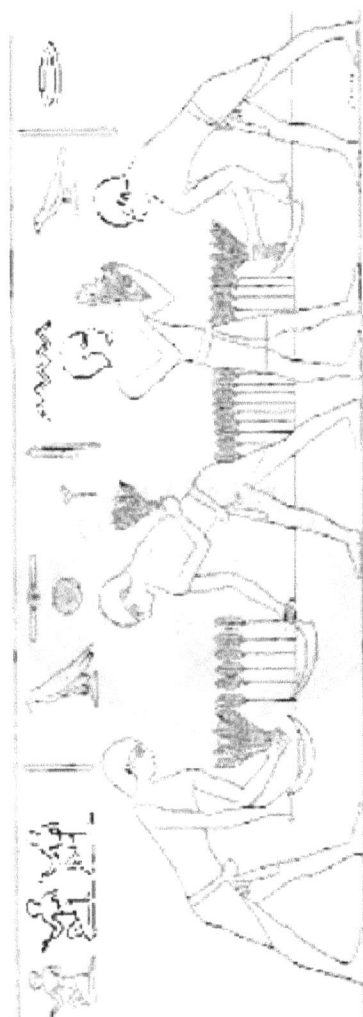

Harvest scene; from a tomb at Gizeh.   (Champollion, pl. 417.)

about this sickle.   You no doubt notice that it is like

a jawbone ; well that is exactly what it originated from.
But the time is so remote when real jawbones were
used as scythes, that even these labourers of 3000 years
ago do not know the origin of their present implement.

Milking-time ; from the tomb of Menofee, at Sakkarah.
(Champollion, pl. 408.)

Only you and I can look over their shoulder into a still
more distant past, and, seeing that "jawbone" and
"scythe" continued to have but one name through all
those ages, we can understand what *might* be meant,
when we read that Samson slew his thousands with the
jawbone of an ass.

CHAPTER V.

UR— Babylon—Nineveh, these are what I have to show you now.

Are there any other cities in all the earth that you

Mount at Mugheir ("Ur" of the Chaldees).

would rather see? I think not. Ur of the Chaldees, whence Abraham the faithful set out on his strange journey at the command of Jehovah; Babylon, the

mighty, the fallen, whose name and whose fate have
been burnt into our very hearts by the scathing words
of priest and prophet; Nineveh, the home of Sennacherib and his hosts, the last royal residence of the
sons of Asshur.

We have crossed the Red Sea, leaving Egypt far behind us on the west, and now we stand on a vast plain,
among the lost cities and silent dwellings of Mesopo-

Interior of Mesopotamian house.

tamia. But the dead shall live again, and a thousand
voices shall speak to us to-day from the sculptured
walls and stoney books of men who have preceded us
into the Great Hereafter by thirty centuries or more.
The cloud which obscures the dawn of civilization is
denser here than in the "Lotus Land"; we can neither
see so far nor so much. Egypt has already opened
with lavish hand her long-locked storehouses; but the
day is not far off when the magic wand of science shall

wile from Assyria, too, her treasured secrets, and they
shall be an open page, in a language which every nation
under heaven may read.   We are even now face to face
with mighty hunters and warrior kings who but yesterday were as shadows ; for Nebuchadnezzar reigns again
in Babylon—Sennacherib in Nineveh.

Their country is only a narrow strip, yet it stretches
for more than 500 miles to north and south, with the
Euphrates on one side and the Tigris on the other.   It
seems to divide itself naturally into two parts, the

Gudéa.

" Upper" and the " Lower" lands, and you may call
the whole Mesopotamia, or you may call it Babylonia,
they are one and the same.   Some even call it all
Assyria, but only the upper part should be so named,
while the lower may be either Babylonia, Chaldea, or
Lower Mesopotamia.

There, immediately before you, is Chaldea, and the
mount, at the foot of which you stand, though now
called Mugheir, is really Ur.   This, and the adjoining
cities of Erech, Eridhu, Larsam, and Sirgulla are the

most ancient in all Mesopotamia, and I could show you
many strange things in each of them. Here, for example, is the head of a prince named Gudea, who ruled
in Sirgulla 5000 years ago at the very least, and
whose title of "Patesi," or priest-king, is of greater
antiquity than any other you have ever heard of. In
early days the people dwelt in tents, or in huts built of
the enormous reeds which are so plentiful here. The
roofs were arched over and covered with rush-mats,

Hebrew dwelling in Mesopotamia.

for in Chaldea is neither wood nor stone, and to
bring these from distant countries is too laborious and
too costly to be often attempted. The few tree-trunks
that ever came in the way of an enterprising Chaldean
are utilized as columns and rafters in the most recherché
dwellings. But such primitive structures would not do
at all for temples of gods and palaces of kings; so, as
their eyes fell on the clay with which their huts were
plastered, the idea arose of forming cakes which should
resemble stones.

Thus men began to make bricks. At first they were rude and perishable, crumbling away in the sun and dissolving in the rain. Then somebody thought of baking them, but as this proved expensive, the economical Chaldee continued to use unbaked bricks for the inner part of his walls, and contented himself with a facing of baked ones for the exterior. The latter were now splendidly made, and no doubt intended to last for ever; so each was stamped, as in Egypt, with

Brick from Erech.

the name of the reigning king, that there might be no mistake about its age and origin. Here is one from Erech, made so long ago that even those wedge-shaped characters we have become so familiar with in Assyria were only beginning to evolve out of the yet more remote picture-writing of Accad.

I want you to notice what a horror the ancient Chaldean has of anything like a curve. Even the sun, which you might think every sane person would represent as round, is here depicted as a lozenge. I can't explain it, but a curve, in the opinion of the early Chaldean scribe, is a thing to be eschewed. The artist is not above using the objectionable form, but the architect takes after the scribe, so rectangular houses and square towers are quite *de rigeur* in Babylonian cities. You grumbled at the lighting arrangements of the Egyptians—honest people!—but you might very well have kept that for the present occasion. A loop-hole here and there you may see in Assyrian habitations; a window, never! They have, however, two peculiar methods of interior decoration which are used by nobody else I ever heard of. One is to form patterns by pushing cones of coloured terra-cotta into the walls while these are still soft. The broad ends of the cones appear in the design like a series of round studs. The other method is to use little clay cups in a similar way; the hollow part being kept to the front gives the

Terra-cotta Cone.

Jar Coffin from Ur. (Taylor.)

walls a curious honeycombed effect.   One of the cores is
lying beside you, and the extraordinary object next it
is a coffin, which reminds me that nothing is stranger
about these Chaldeans than their burial customs.
Northward, in Assyria, you will not find the vestige of
a tomb, and you actually wonder whether they ever
died at all; but here you find the dead heaped up in

Dish-cover Coffin, Mugheir.   (Taylor.)

inconceivable numbers, and there is no cemetery in the
world—except Memphis, perhaps—to compare with
that of Erech.   For miles the coffins are not merely
laid side by side, but are piled one above another, down
to a depth of nearly sixty feet.   The people have no
fancy for the tedious process of embalming, and simply
pack their departed relations either into bottles, like
the one before you, or into an equally incomprehensible
sort of stone slipper; or else they lay them away on a

slab of baked brick, and put a huge terra-cotta "dish-cover" over them.

There is another thing I must tell you—the people in this locality do not believe in climbing stairs. You will notice that the houses have only one storey, and even in this lofty stronghold, which is built exactly like the royal palaces both of Babylon and Nineveh, there is no attempt at more than one floor. Land is cheap, and where a large train of followers has to be housed, the dwelling simply spreads itself over a larger area.

Interior of a Chaldean Tomb.

Do not, however, run away with the idea that there are no stairs in Babylonia; you find them *outside* and not inside the buildings, that is all. The sanctuaries at the summits of those square towers—which may either be temples or observatories, and are probably both—can only be reached by outside stairs, winding round and round from base to apex.

As you move on to Babylon you are struck with the awful solitude that prevails. The land is water-bound and richer even than Egypt, for it has not one, but two gracious rivers for its dower. Once the vast plains were fed by a wonderful system of watercourses from these parent streams; the land brought forth a hundred fold, aye, three hundred fold, and there was corn and wine in abundance for every man. The Garden of Eden may well be looked for here, because "Eden"

Assyrian stronghold.

was the earliest name of the whole plain, and you will see that these ancient people had their creation and deluge stories ages before Moses was born to write the version you know so well. They had their "tree of life," the "Holy Pine-tree," in the midst of the garden, and many a fine poem and sculptured group still exists to commemorate these things. Yet behold now the land has become a desert, and her cities heaps; Babylon is a reproach and a byword. The rude walls of the goat-herd's hut bear everywhere the royal seal of Nebuchadnezzar; for the palaces of the kings are

The Tower of the Seven Planets at Dur-Sargina (after Place).

brickfields, and a new race has built new cities with the bricks thereof. Now and then a green patch refreshes your eye; all else is wilderness, sorrowful in its terrible desolation. The sombre pile of El Heimar looms in the eastern distance; across the Euphrates rises Birs Nimrud, and between these the river wends its silent course to the sea. It has on

K

easy-going temper, this Euphrates ; and steals sleepily
enough through the sandy valley : but the Tigris is an

The Garden of Eden. A roller die from Ohaldea
(plane development).

Brick inscribed "Nebuchadnezzar, King of Babylon, Restorer
of the pyramid and the Tower.   Eldest son of Nabopolassor,
King of Babylon."

impatient, excitable thing, and hurries by fits and
starts along its narrow bed, until all at once it settles

down and weds its gentle neighbour. For many a year
they fought shy of each other; growing unconsciously
every day nearer for all that; still, they might never
have come together, but that the friendly sea lent a
helping hand, discreetly creeping farther and farther
back as they approached, and
refusing to give them sanc-
tuary until they were one.
So the match was made at
last, and in the evening of
their days they travel by one
channel to their common goal.

As you move on to Babylon
you see that through the very
heart of the city flows Euphrates the beautiful, spanned
by a stupendous bridge having
a royal palace on either extremity, and on the western
side the temple of the great
god, Bel. The city is square;
its walls measure fifteen miles
on every side, and there are
twenty-five brazen gates by
which you may enter. Let us
go in by the nearest one.

What a number of gods
these people have. Images
and altars of Bel, Dagon,
Ashtoreth, and Assur meet

Anu or Dagon; the fish-
god.

you wherever you turn, and are supplemented by an
even greater list of demons. If all tales be true, the
evils which the latter are continually devising, must
make the life of the unlucky Babylonian perfectly
intolerable at times. Witches too are plentiful, and
like those in our own nursery days, they take their
evening constitutional through the air on broomsticks !

But Chaldean magic is of world-wide fame, and many are the charms against those evil spirits. There is a bit of necromancy going on behind you at this very minute. That young girl has been smitten by plague, of course some demon is at the bottom of it, so the parents bring her to the priest, who looks through his books for a formula which shall meet the case. Ah! he has found one, and we will take the liberty of

Altar

reading it over his shoulder, while he gets his materials into order.

"Arrange flat in regular bands on the left, a woman's diadem: divide it twice in seven little bands: gird the forehead with it; gird his hands and his feet: set him on his bed and pour on him enchanted waters. Let the disease be carried away into the heavens like a violent wind; may the earth swallow it up like passing waters."

He proceeds to carry out these rather complicated

instructions by winding a long cloth band round the
invalid's body, tying it in seven knots each time.
The application of holy water, and the fastening of a
sentence from a good book round the forehead follows,
while an amulet tied round the neck infallibly pro-
tects her from further attacks.

Priest in his Tabernacle.

Now, I know you want to see what the magician has
written on these charms. Well, on one are the words,
" The demon who seizes man; the Gigim who works
evil: Spirit of the Heavens, conjure it ! Spirit of the
Earth, conjure it ! " The sentence on the forehead
says, " May a ray of peace shine upon her and cure the

disease." It is to be hoped the maiden will find these incantations efficacious, for they are all the treatment

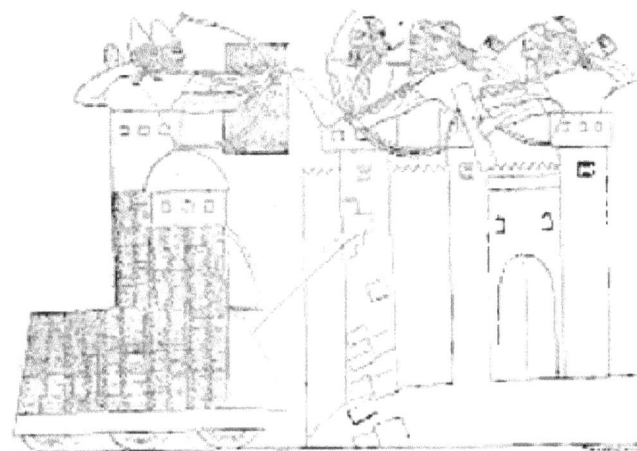

The Battering Rams opening the breach in the wall.

she will receive. wily Chaldee does

Assyrian standard.

I may whisper, however, that the not trust solely to the *words* of his formulæ; that enchanted water is really a very valuable infusion of medicinal herbs, but he takes care to keep his patient in the dark about that, so the credit of the cure is placed to magic, not medicine.

I am afraid I must carry you off now, for we should have been at Nineveh long before this time of day. We are in Assyria proper now, and a lively spot it is. The prevailing occupation is war, and everywhere you see battering rams, fortresses, armies, captives, till you wonder how in the world these sons

of Nimrod ever find time for
their other hobby—the chase.
Yet they are the lion-hunters
of antiquity. As you might
expect, their dogs are carefully
tended. Here is one from the
royal kennel; "Tear-the-foe"

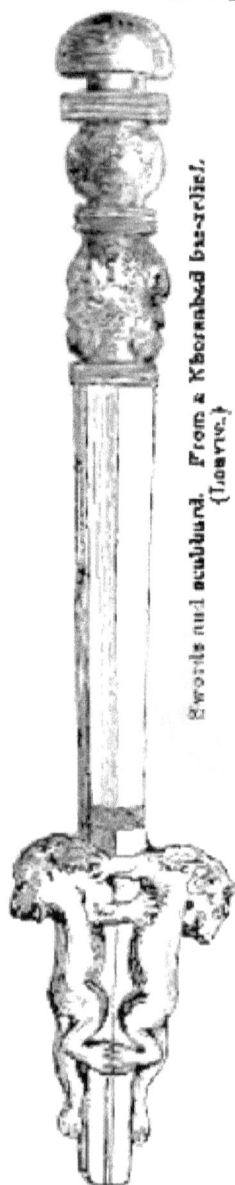

Swords and scabbard. From a Khorsabad bas-relief.
(Louvre.)

Sword scabbard. From the
reliefs. (From Layard.)

is his name, and he looks as if
he could do it too! As it is not
always convenient to hunt the
king of beasts in his native
haunts, a number are kept in
stock, and let out of their cages
to be hunted as required; a

right royal *bellow* you must admit! The Assyrian artist has the chance of studying his lions from nature, and he does not let his opportunities slip.

The lion forms the theme of every conceivable decoration, but I have often wondered how many of the people who have admired the colossal proportions of those winged warders at the palace gates, ever detected the trick the artist has played them. From whichever way you look the creature has its full complement of legs,

Assyrian dog (British Museum).

but to arrive at this, the artist has given him *five*, and the effect from one point of view is peculiar. Perhaps it is on the same principle, that as you cannot see both sides of a cow at once, he has restricted this inoffensive animal to one horn! By-the-bye, I had better explain that those immense ears of corn behind the cows, represent a complete wheat-field. A good deal of valuable time is saved by this little manœuvre, you observe.

Many kings have reigned in Assyria, but we must pass them all over till we come to one called Sargon. He was the second of that name, and like the first was "the son of no man;" yet with him began a new

Lion coming out of his cage. Height of relief about 23 inches. (British Museum.) Drawn by Saint-Elme-Gautier.

dynasty, the most powerful, and the most ill-fated in Assyrian annals. The majority of previous kings had

neglected Nineveh, and spent their money and their time
in military pursuits elsewhere. Sargon and Sennacherib, his son, are of another way of thinking : they are
builders as well as warriors, and the latter has not
only restored the quays and ramparts of Nineveh, but

Lion from the palace of Assurnasirpal, Nimroud.
(British Museum.)

built the splendid palace you see there; and the city is
once more the royal residence of the kings of Assyria.
Higher and higher rises the empire under Essarhaddon
and Assurbanipal (Sardanapalus), the son and grandson
of Sennacherib, until her glory and her pride are by-

words among the nations, just as, in days to come, shall be her everlasting overthrow. Sargon has built himself a city and a palace close to Nineveh, and they are marvels of architectural beauty; he called them by his own name, but nowadays the people call the place Khorsabad. The gate before you is the one used on state occasions, and close by is that of the harem. Sargon is blest with three wives, and, as might be expected, there are frequent bickerings among these ladies, so the sorely beset husband builds a distinct suite of apart-

Assyrian cows. (National Library, Paris.)

ments for each, and thus ensures some degree of domestic peace. On state occasions the reigning favourite ventures to invite her lord to a banquet, and gets herself up for the ordeal regardless of expense. Her jewellery is massive enough for a cyclops, but in most cases is well designed. I must protest against the size of the child's head on those earrings, though!

The pendants of the necklace are all sacred symbols; most of them old friends; the lotus, however, is not included. The embroidery on Assurbanipal's mantle is well worth looking at, and before leaving the banqueting room you must examine the goblets and spoons, as

The Royal Palace of Sennu.   From Perrot and Chipiez.

One of the gates of the city of Sargon.

Triumphal gate at the entrance to the palace.   From Place.

well as the platters; the latter are made after a distinctly
Egyptian pattern.   Here is the bedroom of one of the
royal dames; rather comfortless we would find it, but
there is nothing to complain of as regards stability.
The Egyptians may excel as builders of stone; the
Assyrians are unsurpassed in the magnitude of their

Winged bull from the gate.

brickwork: the former are pre-eminent for artistic
finish; the latter for vigour of conception.   At the
same time they came a good deal in contact, and each
has had a certain influence on the other.   Look at the
decoration of this arched Assyrian gateway and compare it with that bit of painting from Thebes; they
are almost identical.   Here, on the other side, is an

arch which is quite Assyrian in character: the cable
and rosette are especially favoured by Assyrian artists.
But after all, what you have come to Nineveh to see

One of the gates of the harem at Sargon. From Place.

are not buildings, but books—books the oldest the
world possesses, the most interesting ever written.
Stories more ancient by far than even the vener-

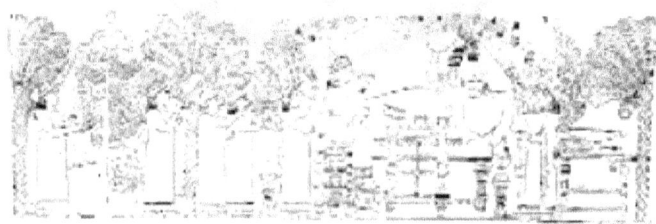

Assurbanipal drinking with the Queen.

able Genesis histories you have read so often.
They are not books of paper remember, not even of
papyrus; they are all of stone or hard clay. Many

have been broken, and there are, alas! many leaves missing; but you have only to place the precious fragments side by side with your own Bible story, and something like awe fills your soul as you confess that at last you have found the originals of the oldest chapters

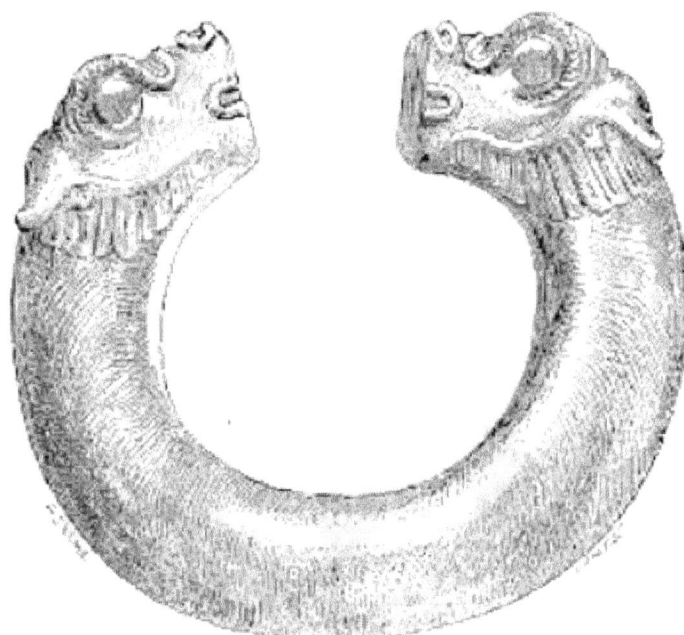

Bronze bracelet.   Diameter 5 inches.   (Louvre.)   Drawn by
Saint-Elme Gautier.

of earth's oldest book.   Here are the royal libraries of Nineveh—of Sennacherib, in fact, and of his son Assurbanipal.   Come with me, and I will show you the books.

There were at one time over 30,000 of them, but as I said before, many are gone.   Every subject is treated in these stone volumes—law; mythology; grammar; history; mathematics; astronomy.

They are of all sizes, from a square inch to a square

Gold earring. (British Museum.)

Royal necklace. From Rawlinson.

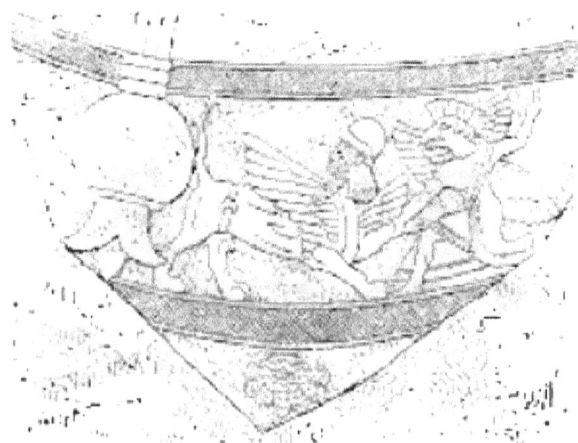

Detail of embroidery on the king's robe. From Layard.

foot, and they are of many ages; for Assurbanipal, not content with what his own savants produced, sought through all the land for tablets which were antiquities even in his day, nearly 3000 years ago; and so

L

gathered together the literary treasures of Ur, Larsa and every ancient city into this wonderful library at Nineveh.

This is a piece of the deluge tablet, very much broken, you see; still, the text is plain enough. I will read you some of the lines. "To

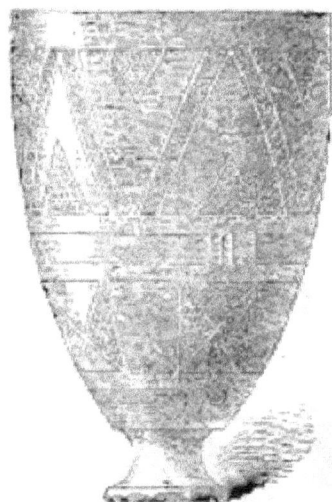

Goblet. Height 5 inches.
(Louvre.)

make a deluge the great gods have wrought their heart. ... Man of Surippak, make a ship, and cause the seed of life of every kind to go up into it. The ship thou shalt make—GOO cubits its measure in length. .... 60 cubits the amount of its breadth and height." Then the story goes

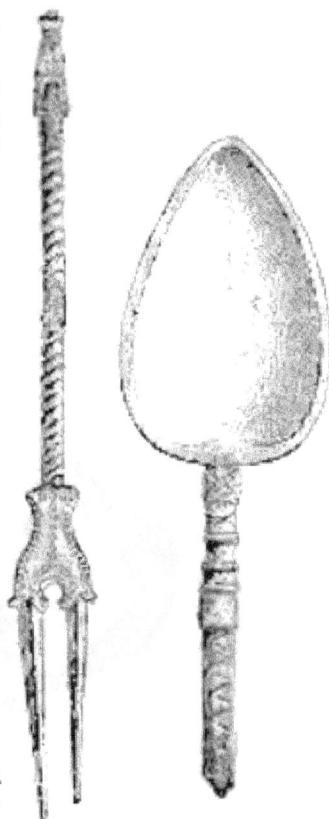

Bronze fork and spoon. From Smith's *Assyrian Discoveries*.

on to tell how, after the ship is built, Xisuthros, the
Babylonian Noah, enters; and how he and his family

Part of the Deluge tablet.

alone survive the deluge. A dove, and then a swallow
are sent forth, but each returns; a little later and a
raven leaves the ark, and is no more seen.

L 2

The deluge is past. Xisuthros descends from the ark, and, behold, a rainbow appears as token of future safety. Like Enoch, the patriarch is at last translated: the people gaze with rapt eyes on his receding form

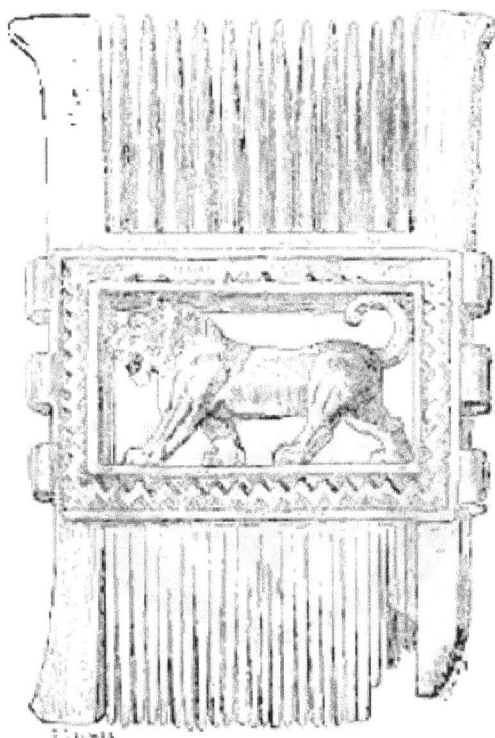

Ebony comb.   Actual size.   (Louvre.)

till cloud and mist envelop it. Then they take counsel together; they too would be immortal; so they essay to build a tower that shall rise to heaven. But, suddenly, in the night, comes a mighty wind; their tower is overthrown, their language confounded,

and they themselves are scattered to the four corners
of the earth. The creation story, too, is here, and is
in many volumes. One of them tells you that "Anu

A bedroom in the harem at Sargon.

made suitable the mansions of the great gods. The
stars he placed in them, the moon-god he caused to
beautify the thick night . . . and the sun to be on the

horizon at its rising." Another relates how "the gods
created the living creatures. . . . They made the living
beings come forth, the cattle of the field, the beast of
the field, and the creeping thing." Is not this all very
familiar to you? Did I not speak truly when I said

Fragment of a threshold; from Khorsabad.   (Louvre.)
Drawn by Bourgoin.

you would find in Nineveh the first beginnings of an
old, old story?

What a variety of books there is; but then everybody can read and write in Babylonia. Clay is
plentiful, and clay is the Babylonian's writing-paper,

so there is no excuse for the man who cannot sign his
own name. Every city has its free library, and even
the king's brother does not disdain the office of librarian.
The books are all numbered and arranged in order, and
the rules enjoin every student to give the librarian

Door ornament; from Kouyundjik. After Rawlinson.

notice in writing of the volume he wishes to read.
Just glance at some of these legal tablets.

Most interesting of them all, perhaps, is the private
will of Sennacherib. It is too long for you to stay
to decipher now; I may whisper, however, that it
makes full provision for the king's favourite son, Essar-

huddou, to the displenishment of the other scious of the royal house, and considerable uncharitableness will be displayed when it comes to bo read, I should think!

From the private will of Sennacherib (700 B.C.).

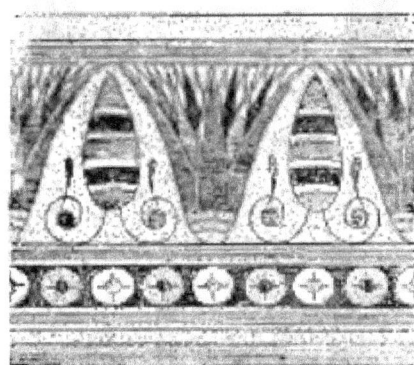

Painted border; from Thebes. After Prisse.

The married women's property act is fully enforced, luckily for her; for her husband can turn her adrift at

any moment by paying a small fine into court; while she,
poor soul, finds a watery grave should she attempt to

Detail of enamelled archevolt. Khorsabad. From Place.

separate herself from an undesirable partner! The
judges are everywhere admonished to beware of

bribery! Property is carefully protected, and though slaves are held, they may purchase their freedom if they wish. Rich men let out their land to market-gardeners, the tenant giving one-third of the produce as rent; and you may have the house (furnished) on lease if you like. It seems really cheaper to buy than to lease, however, for here are the deeds of a house purchased in Nineveh 2500 years ago for one maneh of silver (9*l.*). The Sabbath is religiously observed, and the Assyrians must neither cook any food nor change their dress on that day. They are even cautioned against taking advantage of the day of rest to indulge in a dose of medicine!

Ivory tablet of Egyptian design.

The science par excellence of Assyria is astronomy. Observatories are established in convenient localities, and every fortnight a report goes to the government from the Astronomer-Royal. This tablet came from Larsem; on it square and cube roots are calculated correctly from one to sixty, and there is a series of geometrical

Ivory panel. Actual size. (British Museum.)

figures strongly suggestive of a Babylonian Euclid.
A poet-laureate, too, is established at Nineveh, and,
not long ago, I saw a deed duly signed and sealed,
bestowing on this wide-awake individual a handsome
piece of land, in acknowledgment of some unusually
complimentary verses to the king. Here is the signet
of Sennacherib himself, not the usual flat seal we use,

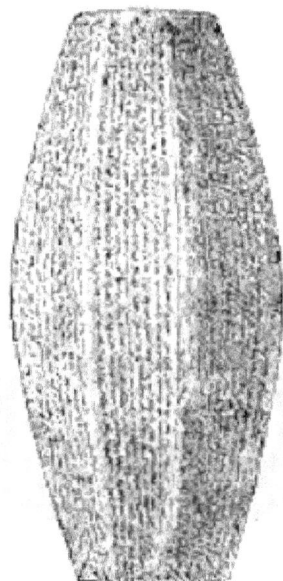

A book from the royal library at Nineveh.

but a little cylinder of green feldspar, which, when
rolled on the soft clay tablets, gives this impression.
Everybody uses these seals, and some of them remind
you strongly of our old friends the bronze and iron
men. This one bears both sun and moon symbols, and
next it is another having a curious monster, with goat's
head and fish's tail, on the sacrificial altar. This last

belongs to a banker of Babylon, and has been impressed

Part of a bronze Cup or plaster. Illuminine about B.C. 1500. (British Museum.)

on a contract tablet, dated "the twelfth year of Darius,
king of Babylon, king of the Nations." All sorts and

sizes of cylinder seals are lying about, some of them very archaic; and, in addition, there are several which resemble our own flat ones.

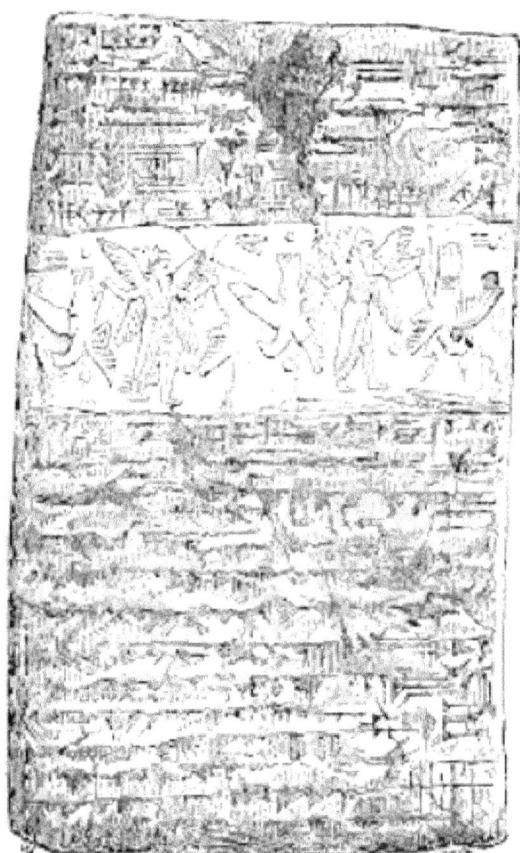

Tablet with impression from a cylinder.   From Layard.

You might examine these treasures for many hours, and not exhaust them; but it is already late, and we are still far from the top of our street. The bank is

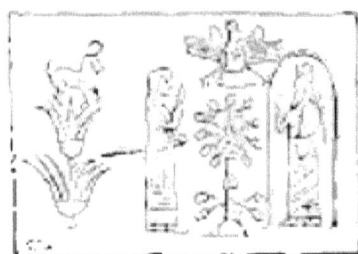

The seal of Sennacherib. (Cylinder of green feldspar in the British Museum.)

Chaldæan cylinder. From Ménant.

Impression from the same cylinder.

Chaldæan cylinder dating from the second monarchy. Black jasper. (British Museum.)

just over yonder, but we can't stop to look in. It is
conducted very similarly to those you are accustomed
to see, only that the deeds are kept in jars instead of
safes. Interest to-day is four per cent., but it may
drop to three per cent. to-morrow.

Impression of a cylinder on a contract.   From Ménant.

Farewell, proud Nineveh! We turn away sorrow-
fully, knowing that, before many days, thy queenly
heart will lie in the dust, and no man will regard it.

The day has come—is gone—and Nineveh is dead.

Agate cone.   (National Library, Paris.)

How she met her fate is time's own eternal secret.
Some say that fire consumed her, others, that the
Tigris played the traitor, and broke a passage-way for
her bitterest foe. One thing is sure—Nineveh is
wiped from off the face of the earth, and that suddenly; and with her has passed the empire of Asshur.

CHAPTER VI.

A REGION OF PALM.

ANYTHING more insignificant than the scrap of country we have stumbled into now could scarcely be imagined. But size doesn't count for much in the character of a country—as you ought to know, if anybody does—and the gentlemen who own this boxed-in strip of sand have managed somehow to place both themselves and their land on a very high pinnacle of respectability indeed. Of course, they ought to have been here to receive us, but they are nothing of the kind, and, as a matter of fact, it is their very gadding propensities that have been the making of them. They have completely outwitted the propounder of the old adage; and, as rolling stones, have been an unqualified success.

Long, long ago, a party of travellers from the other side of the street chanced to run into this district just as you and I have done to-day. They had never seen anything like the groves of palms which covered it right down to the water's edge, and when they returned to their own country they had no other name by which to distinguish the land they had seen than "Phœnicé"; "the country where the palms grow." They came to know it well enough later on however, for, octopus-like, the men of Phœnicé stretched out an arm on the smallest provocation, and grabbed whatever and wherever they could. So the palm waves over many a dwelling besides those in front of you, and we shall

M

have a pretty brisk time of it chasing the adventurers
from one to another of their manifold colonies.   We

Descent from the Pass of Legnia, in the Lebanon

must, in duty bound, see what they have to show us at home, however, before we follow them abroad; so push your way through the belt of palms and come with me into the fertile plain beyond. The air is laden with the fragrance of orange blossoms, and the landscape glows with scarlet pomegranate flowers, and autumn-tinted vine leaves. The sea still lies on our western side, and dimly in the east you see the cedar-clad slopes and snowy summit of the great "White Mountain," which is Lebanon.

We stand between two families of palm-growers—two groups of dwellings, each having a world-wide reputation. Each demands a share of our patronage, and all we have to decide is which to take first. In one case the entire population has turned out on some important work. That settles it; inquisitiveness demands that we at once proceed to the scene of action, so turn your steps to the southward please, and make your first acquaintance with the city of —— no, on second thoughts, you shall have a little conundrum this time, and find out the name of this place for yourself—if you can! It is the city of "pleasant houses," and these rise, story after story, in a way that would have made an Assyrian architect shudder. Here are temples and dwellings as beautiful as any you have ever seen; yonder is the royal palace, and this is the grand square of the town. The people are all crowded on the beach or are lying out to sea in boats, and far too busy to notice us, but when we reach them you will be more inclined to watch them than quarrel with their apparent inhospitality. Over the sides of every boat are cast long ropes with baskets attached at close intervals; all among the shallow, rocky creeks nearer the shore, Tom, Dick, and Harry are grubbing about as if for a wager. There is no doubt about it, they are perfectly delighted with what they find, but you look for half an hour and never catch the glint of a silvery scalo: it is most exasperating; what in the world are

Ancient Phœnician house. From Houel.

they chuckling over? Patience, my dear sir; they
have evidently got as much of their invisible merchan-

diss as they can carry, and are about to come ashore.
Well, I never was so disappointed in my life. Pockets-
ful; creelsful; whole ship-loads of—winkles! Nothing
else. But are they winkles? Look again. You superciliously turn one or two of the horrid little molluscs
over with your toe and conclude that there is something
strange about them. Ah, one of the boatmen informs

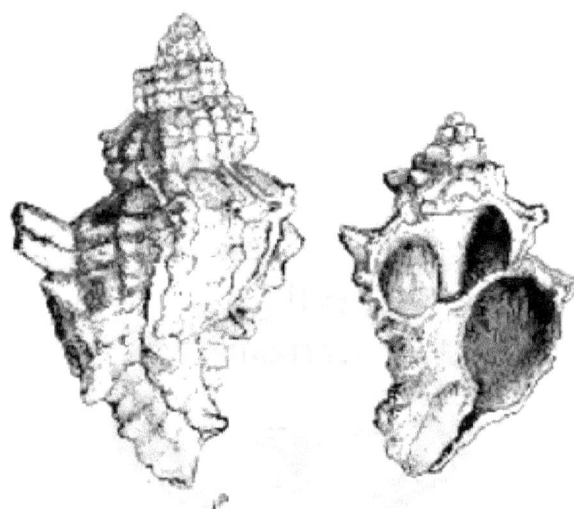

The Murex trunculus. From Lortet.

me they are the *Purpura pelagia* or *Murex trunculus*,
and the *Purpura lapillus* or *Buccinum lapillus*. I had
intended to inquire what they were a pint, and whether
he had a pin handy, for though I am not partial to a
fish diet myself. I know somebody who is. But there;
it gives me quite a turn to think how nearly I put my
foot in it; the bare idea of attacking the *Purpura
pelagia (Murex trunculus)* with a pin! I'd rather not
venture any more questions, thank you, but we will

follow the crowd at a respectable distance and find out
what they mean to do with the creatures, all the same;
I am more curious than ever.

We seem to be entering a sort of factory, and as the
fishermen empty out their baskets of precious *Murex*
and *Buccinum*—don't ask me to repeat the whole
appellations—each wretched mollusc is killed by a
single blow. It is instantly dissected and a sac or vein
which begins at the head and continues throughout the
entire spiral anatomy, is carefully removed. The contents of this vein are yellowish-white and creamy in
consistence, but when exposed to light become first
green, then purple. No reason can be found for the
existence of this substance in the animal; it is never
exuded, as cuttle-fish exude sepia. We shall see by-
and-by to what use the men of Phœnice put it.
When removed from the *Murex* the colour-sac is thrown
into a cauldron, but the unfortunate *Buccinum* comes
off much the worse of the two, for, being small, the sac
is not removed, and shell and fish are crushed up
together. While this barbarous process is going on,
the workmen carry in immense vessels of salt, twenty
ounces of which to every hundred pounds of fish are
poured into that great vat. The whole is then left to
macerate for three days. Now pass into the next room
and see the continuation of the manufacture.

This mass has already undergone its three days'
soaking, and is stewing gently in a lead vessel by the
aid of a pipe from an adjoining furnace; brass and iron
vessels are rigidly excluded, as they spoil the colour of
the concoction. The liquor will be simmered and
skimmed, and skimmed and simmered for ten days: it
will then be clear, but sadly diminished in quantity;
eight thousand pounds of pulp only yielding five
hundred pounds of clear liquid. Now they are going
to test the tint: too pale, is it? very well, that simply
means a little more stewing. The colour of the *Bucci-*

rum is not so rich as that of the *Murex*, but the latter

Remains of the walls of Sidon. From Hessin.

is really almost too deep to be beautiful, so it is the
custom to apply the two separately, and the colour

produced is an exquisite purple of the richest tone.
Have you not by this time guessed where you are?
Where but in Tyre can these wonderful dye-works,
this imperial purple be found? They are the boast of
Phœnicia, and though Tyrian purple is imitated at
many places, the imitations never approach the loveli-
ness of the original.

If Tyre is famous for her purple dye, Sidon is no less
so for glass, but it is curious that while the whole
coast from Tyre to Sidon—and the two cities are
twenty miles apart—abounds with the fine white sand

Ruin in the neighbourhood of Sidon.   From Raman.

which is a necessary ingredient in glass, the no less
indispensable alkali is totally absent. It is more by
good luck than good guiding that the Sidonians have
discovered the value of their inexhaustible sand supply.
This is how it happened. A band of Phœnician mer-
chants sailing along the coast with a cargo of soda for
the Syrian soap-boilers, went ashore one day in search
of provisions. There was no trouble in finding materials
for a feast, but the cooking was another matter. In
the shelter of an old ruin a blazing fire was soon made,
but every time the pot was set upon it, the green wood
gave up the ghost, and the hungry sailors were nearly

Necklace of gold and glass. (British Museum.)

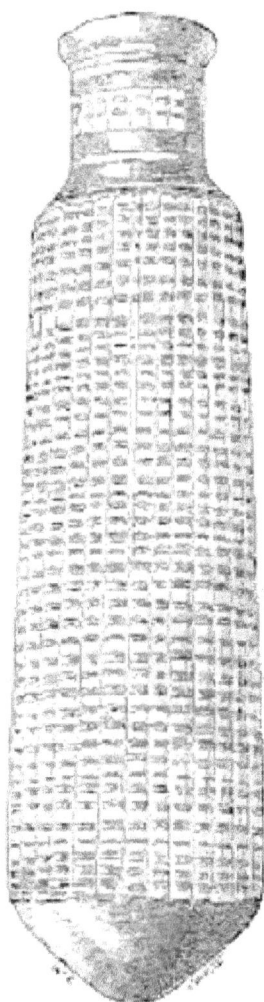

Bottle in the Gréau Collection. Height 7 inches.

desperate, when the genius of the party suggested bringing blocks of soda from the ship to prop the pot up. It was a grand success, and in less than no time the dinner sent a most appetizing aroma from the stew-pan to the nostrils of the impromptu cooks. But the heat was intense, and the natrum blocks began to melt and unite with the sand on which they stood. To the amazement of the onlookers, out of these strange materials came a beautiful, brilliant stream of transparent glass!

And the old Sidonians have profited by the hint the gods have sent them, though they haven't found it all plain sailing, I can tell you. But they are people of no little backbone, and have battled with their difficulties like men. I am bound to admit to you, however, that the Sidonians are not the only discoverers of glass. The Egyptians learnt the secret ages before, and without doubt the later men, having once grasped the great idea, take many a hint from the Land of the Lotus. Blue is the

favourite colour in Phœnicia, as in both Egypt and
Assyria, and besides vases and jars of every shape,
the most beautiful beads and imitations of precious
stones are made. Here is a necklace, a few beads
and the pendants of which are gold; all the rest is

Glass pendant and plaque with sphinx.

Glass plaques and tablets.

glass. The curious little tablets close by are not so
easily accounted for—they tell me the Syrian and
Sidonian ladies sew them upon their gowns; certainly
they have holes pierced through them quite convenient
for sewing, so I suppose it must be true, but they will

give a strange labelled effect to the damsels and their
toggery, I should imagine.

As jewellers and metal-workers, Tyre and Sidon rank
nearly equal. Every great hunting expedition and
petty street scrimmage offers a theme for the engraver.
See, from yonder castle the master is just starting for
the forest : he mounts his chariot, and over his head is
held an umbrella, symbol of his high rank. He sights
a stag upon the hillside, and, leaving his servant with
the chariot, creeps softly behind a tree, and down goes
the stag with an arrow in his brain. There is a feast
in the woods, the stag forming the chief dish ; over-
head the palms wave, the chariot stands in the background, pole up, and the horses enjoy the juicy grass
as the hunter, seated now on a rural throne, and still
protected by his umbrella, invokes the blessing of sun
and moon gods upon the banquet. At last all are
rested, and the journey home begins. An unpleasant
addition to the party appears in the shape of an
immense ape. He makes for the master with the
evident intention of dining off him ; the servants
fly ; another instant and his lordship's hunting days
will be over, when behold, down sweeps the deity so
recently invoked, and off go hunter, chariot and all,
through the air. At a safe distance they alight, but
the hunter has gathered his breath by this time and
goes for Master Monkey tooth and nail. In exactly
five minutes the vultures are making short work of all
that is left of that over-bold animal, and our victorious
sportsman returns to his castle with his nose pretty
high in the air. Quite an exciting adventure, and as
the hero is "somebody" in these parts, a bowl is made
to commemorate the event. It is of silver overlaid
with gold, and is nearly eight inches in diameter. Now
read the story round the rim !

In the decoration of another cup you can see how
largely the Egyptians have influenced Phoenician art ;

and only look at that battered medallion; where will you find anything to match it save in the harem of King Khuenaten?

Bowl from Præneste. In the Kircher Collection.

Phœnicia is a rocky spot, and temples, tombs and dwellings, are more often rock-cut than not. The house beside you is cut from one single mass. It is one hundred feet long, nearly one hundred deep, and the

Part of the decoration of a silver cup.   From Griffi

chambers are divided by partition walls of solid rock twenty feet high and thirty-two inches thick.

Sometimes the rock is made the foundation of a structure, and the building proper is erected on the top of that. Even then, the blocks of rock and stone employed are most ponderous, as you see from the city walls we are now standing under. I have enticed you outside the city that I might show you the great cemetery of Sidon. Cemeteries are, as you know, a weak point of

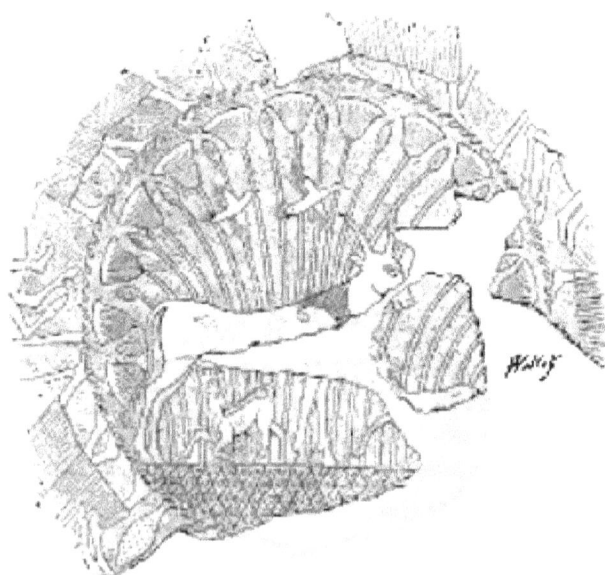

Central medallion from a cap. From Gsell.

mine, and those of Amrit or Marath and of Sidon are the most famous in all Phœnicia. The chambers are underground, and occasionally the old Egyptian well is used, but generally the approach is by a staircase. The grandees repose in splendid marble coffins which often stand in niches all round the tomb-chamber. Here is the sarcophagus of a king of Sidon, who lived and died in perfect terror that one day his last sleep would be disturbed by robbers. Round his coffin is

Rock-cut tombs at Amrit.   From Renan.

inscribed, "Do not open this coffin for the sake of

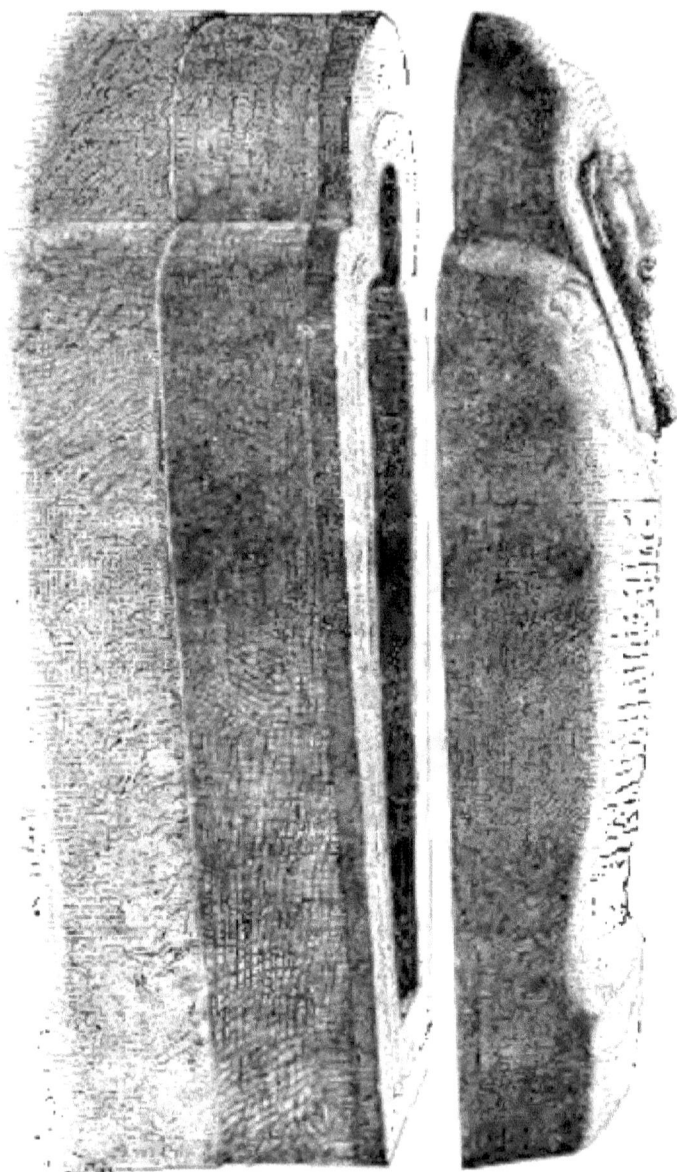

Sarcophagus of Ermouhasut. (Louvre.)

treasure; there are no treasures in it!" Now and then leaden and even sandstone coffins are used, but they

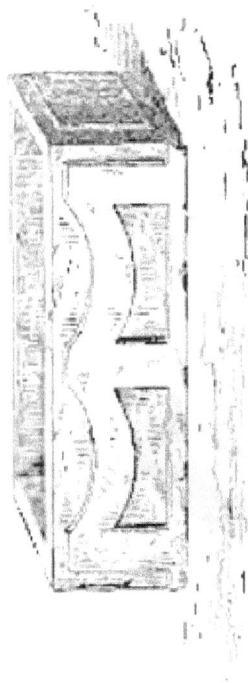

Sandstone coffin. From Heuan.

Leaden coffin. From Lortet.

are not considered *quite* the thing among the *haut ton*. The commonalty neither have coffins nor niches.

They are either placed in carefully-dug graves, or simply laid on the floor on beds of sand. There was a time when cedar coffins came into fashion, but they did

Interior of a tomb at Tharros. From Spano.

not stand the underground climate and were soon abandoned. Cremation never commended itself in the Region of Palm, but the terra-cotta perfume bottles you

N 2

see in nearly every grave show that some attempt was
made to arrest or conceal the natural processes of
decay. Whether the motive was a sanitary one is
another story.

The tombs at Amrit are more roomy than those at
Sidon, but a glance into one must satisfy you. We
have still to visit palm regions that are not Phœnice,
but that yet owe their birth and all that makes them

Tomb at Amrit.   Perspective of Interior.   From Renan.

famous to the sandy little strip between Lebanon and
the sea.

It would be the easiest thing in the world to cross
from here to Cyprus, but if you will take the news
quietly, I will tell you a secret. There is a lady at
Tyre waiting to join us, and we are going back to
pick her up before proceeding on our journey. There,
the murder is out ; you will find her a most agreeable
companion, so no grumbling, but turn round at once,

and as we go I will let you into the private troubles of
the poor woman and explain why I have promised to
get her safely out of Tyre to-day. Her real name is
Elissa, but I know her best as Dido, so you will oblige
me by giving her that appellation also. A good many
years ago her father was King of Tyre, and when he
died he left Dido in charge of her brother Pygmalion,
who is now king. In process of time Dido became a

Model of Phœnician temple in terra-cotta. (Louvre.)
Height 8½ inches.

great beauty and married Acerbas, high priest of
Hercules. This was quite a suitable match, because in
Tyre the priests and Hercules are considered of nearly
equal rank with the king. Acerbas was, besides,
immensely wealthy, and the newly-married pair were
as happy as newly-married pairs usually are.

But Pygmalion is a thoroughly greedy man, and
being determined to possess himself of the treasure of
his sister and her husband, he secretly murdered

Acerbas. Great was his chagrin on finding that the gold for which he had sold his soul had been so cleverly hidden that all his efforts to discover it failed.

For years Dido could not look at her brother, but her life was a sad and dreary one, and at last she determined to leave Tyre and seek forgetfulness in a new land. Moreover, she conceived a plan by which she might escape the snares laid for her by her brother and carry off her money with her. She pretended to be reconciled, and proposed to go and live at the palace

Phœnician merchant galley.   From Layard.

that she might be away from the scene of her sorrow. The king was delighted; if Dido came to his house, so would her belongings, and he has just sent a train of servants to convey both to his royal residence. But Dido has no intention of falling into *that* trap! She has won the servants over to a man, and they have worked like galley-slaves to unearth her treasure and get everything in readiness, and now she, they, and a goodly company of the best and bravest in Tyre only wait to seek with us another and more hospitable home.

Here we are, and here is our good ship ready to lift

The Xanthus Valley.

anchor the moment we are aboard. Everybody else is
here before us, and full of impatience to be off. There is

a nervous apprehension that Pygmalion will give chase,
so, as I remarked before, though nothing would be easier

House at Gheneturu.

them to run across to Cyprus—the earliest offshoot of
the Region of Palm—yet we all agree that to put the
king off the scent we must make a *detour*. So we sail

quickly out to sea and then as quickly turn round and
steer again for the coast, tacking first this way, then
that, till behold, now we are close on the shores of

House at Ghieoben.

Lycia. A Phœnician war-ship is at our heels! Our
little galley has no chance in point of speed; poor
Dido is out of the frying-pan into the fire unless we

Lycian store-room.

can disembark and conceal her and her chattels some-
where in the Lycian territory. Out we bundle and
leave our vessel to its fate. One valley after another

we traverse, passing through village after village in our flight: Xanthus, Patera, Ghendova, Ghiouben. The astonished natives believe us to be a pack of robbers at the very least, and absolutely decline to accommodate us even with a granary to rest in. We

Tomb at Hoiran.

almost decide to take refuge in the tombs at Pinara or Hoiran, which to my mind are a vast deal more inviting than the houses, but, with the usual superstition of sailors, our men refuse to enter any such lodgings, and in desperation we prove our right to the bad name that has been given us by stealing a pair of bullocks

A REGION OF PALM. 127

and an empty cart from a roadside inn. Our worn-out
liege lady is deposited inside with more haste than
ceremony, and we decamp before the awe-stricken

Hut in Lydia.

owner has time to gather his scattered wits about him.
In half an hour we cross the frontier into Phrygia, and

Portrait of King Midas.

at last sit down in security, if not comfort, under the
shadow of the monument of old King Midas.

Midas is a deceased king of Phrygia who was afflicted,
poor soul, with asses' ears. Some kind friend invented

the Phrygian cap which effectually hid this misfortune from the world; but the thing was no secret to one individual: the king's barber could not be cheated. He promised, however, to keep the matter to himself,

Monument of Midas.   False door.   Drawn by R. Coulbourne.

and for a long time so he did. But gradually the impulse to tell somebody became uncontrollable, and the poor man, still faithful to his trust—as he believed—went down to the river banks and relieved his mind by

whispering the secret to the reeds and rushes. In two
days the whole town had it! for the deceitful plants
waved about in the wind from morning till night, calling
out "Midas has asses' ears! Midas has asses' ears!"[5]
Well, poor Midas is out of his misery by this time, and
here is his monument. I am sure we ought to be
obliged to him for having such a nice one. Even our
gallant tars now swallow their scruples, and sagely
remark that a clean, dry grave is better than a damp,
tumble-down wooden house. They won't be put to
the test of proving their words, however, for King

Phrygian house.

Midas' monument lacks one essential; it hasn't a door,
consequently we cannot possibly go inside. No, that
is not a door, or, to be more correct, it is a false one.
Nobody has ever yet found out what lies behind that
rocky barrier, and you and I are not likely to make any
experiments to-day, so, for any real benefit this monument is to us, it might as well not exist.

The houses are abominably draughty; I wonder why
the women do not pin up some of those thick rugs they
are everlastingly weaving. Did you know that some
of the nicest carpets and rugs in the world are made in
Phrygia? Here are the looms: some upright, some

horizontal, but all of the simplest description ; and this
is one of the combs with which the weaver strikes the
warp from top to bottom of the frame when a series of
courses is complete.

I like busy people, but I must say that in Phrygia
they overdo it, and it is cold comfort that tired travellers
like ourselves get in such a place. In fact, it looks
uncommonly like finding our way back to the sea-coast
and committing ourselves once more to the arms of
Neptune. Our route lies through Lydia and Caria,
and though at this hour in the afternoon we shall not

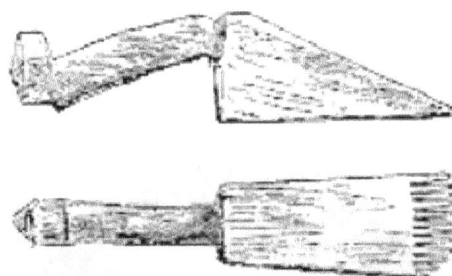

Comb of carpet-maker.

have time to loiter there, you will yet be able to see
something of these outskirts of the Region of Paltu.

The Lydians are the world's first coiners. Even the
cultured dwellers of the Nile never conceived a money
system which would have a fixed acknowledged value.
Ring money you have long ago come across, and latterly
ingots have been used in commercial transactions, but
the difficulties of weighing these, and the settling of
endless disputes arising where merchandise is paid in
kind instead of in coin, have inspired the Lydian king
with the idea of stamping his ingots in such a way as
to give them a definite official value ; so Lydia has set
up the first mint, and yonder are some of the coins.

The king's name is Crœsus : you have probably heard

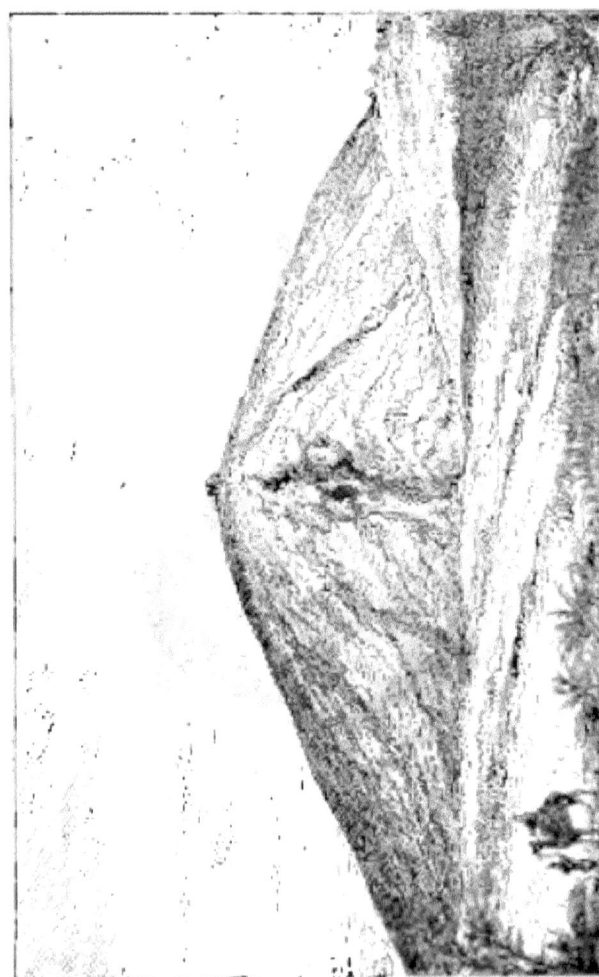

Tomb of Alyattes, father of Crœsus.

of him before, and know that he has made a very tidy
fortune by his business-like habits and improved cur-

rency. We are at this moment passing by the tomb of
his father Alyattes, a very sharp fellow, but not a
patch on Croesus!

Lydian coins.   Electrum.

Lydian plaque.

The invention of coining is the glory of Lydia, but

Crœsus does not confine his metal-work to coins. Here
is a golden plaque for sewing on a dress, which merits
a word of approval from you. There is a touch of
Egypt about it, but you will find our old sun, star and
triangle signs in evidence also. The design is much
enriched by the row of pearls at the edge; the little
loops are for pendants.

And now, this is Caria, famous for potteries. Good
clay is so plentiful that coffins, as well as vases and
cooking-pots, are made of it. The shapes are not bad,

Carian pottery.

but you will see others so much more curious at Cyprus
that you need not trouble to expend your critical
energies here. We hurry on to Halicarnassus, the
great Carian sea-port; and here it is, in the native city
of Herodotus and Dionysius, that we find the most interesting specimens of the dwellings of the country. A
palace built of fine reddish-yellow baked bricks—the
palace of a man whose name will never be forgotten; not
because of any special deed of his, but on account of
a tomb, not yet built, which shall become the pattern

and model of every succeeding age. Halicarnassus is
the home of Mausolus, and at a not far-distant date his
disconsolate widow, Queen Artemisia, will gather around
her the greatest artists at home and abroad to devise
such a monument to dead Mausolus as shall astonish
the whole world.

Oval bottle.   From Cesnola.

From Caria to Cyprus is a pretty stiff pull, but we
are here at last. Is it not aggravating to be told as soon
as we land that all our ignominious dodging of Pygmalion has been perfectly unnecessary, and that instead
of being on our track he has been quietly attending to
his own home affairs ?   Between ourselves, I believe he

did prepare for a chase, but, obedient to the family deity, who cautioned him against doing anything of the kind, he changed his mind and left his sister to

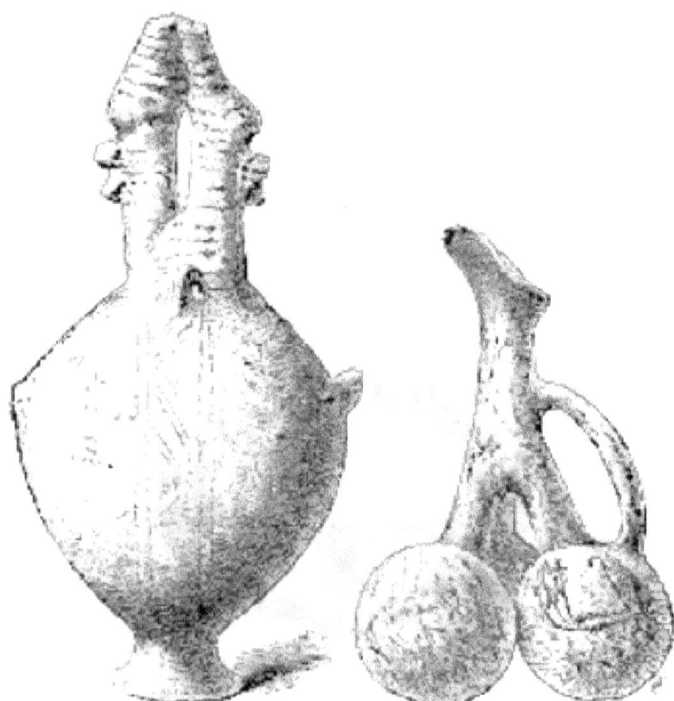

Bottle with double neck.   Bottle with triple body.
(Feuardent collection.)

accomplish her own destiny. She has gone now to consult her patron, Hercules, and we shall take the chance of looking round the famous dockyards of Cyprus in the meantime.

o 2

A whole fleet of ships is being loaded with terra-cotta jars and images! Do step down and see the extraordinary-looking things they are. Here is a bottle with two necks and one body; there is one with

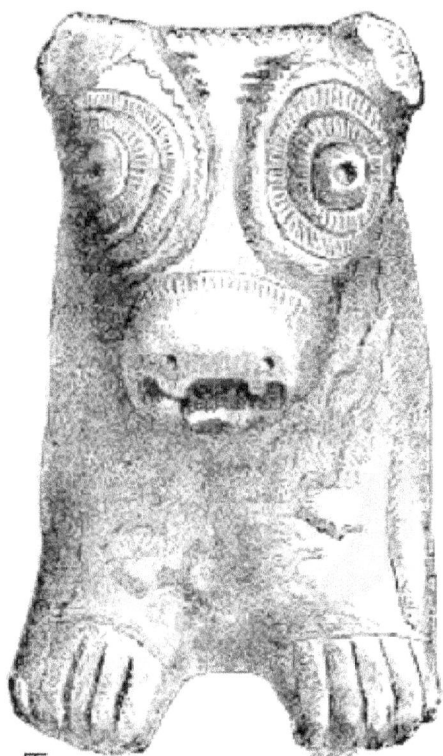

Vessel from Cyprus.

three bodies and one neck! After these comes a perfect menagerie of impossible monsters, and it is quite a relief to turn to the next consignments which, if peculiar, are certainly very cleverly made. Cyprus is liter-

Vessels in the form of quadrupeds.

Vessel in shape of a goat.

Vase in the Piot collection.

ally sown broadcast with crockery of this description,
and if we had time to walk across the island—which
we haven't—you would be charmed with the quaint

The hill of Paphos, remains of a temple in the foreground. PLATE CXXVLIX.

conceits of these old Phœnician colonists. What a
lovely spot it is! I cannot imagine anything finer
than the hill of Paphos right behind us, or the grand

colonnaded tombs at Nea-Paphos, now black with the

Courtyard of a tomb at Nea-Paphos.

smoke of the swine-herds who shelter there, or that
glimpse of the ancient oratory and fountain, the

Panaghía Phanéromeni, where you can just see the

The Panaghia Phaneromeni.

forms of a pair of lovers who go to light a lamp before

the altar.   If, at daybreak, the light still burns, their
felicity is assured, if not—well, I suppose they will try
again some day—with different partners.

But here comes our lady fair.   The gods decree that
she tarry not in Cyprus.   The priest of Hercules himself is now to share her enterprise, for it is ordained
that he and his shall be high priests for ever in the

The wall of Byrsa.

city she is yet to build.   So we hurry off from Cyprus,
taking many maidens to become wives in the new
Region of Palm.

It is a long time before we find a haven again, but
at last the oracle says, " Go now and found a city here."
And Dido consults with the people of the place, and
buys from them as much land as an ox's hide will cover,
so that we may all sit down after our long and weary

journey.   Not much comfort for a hundred people on
six square feet of soil, you think.   We are not quite
ready to sit down, thank you !   when we are, there will
be ample accommodation.   Our ox-hide is no pigmy !
We cut it up into very narrow strips, join them all

Carthaginian cistern walls.

together, and then proceed to enclose the nicest site we
can see.   It is no inconsiderable "intake," I assure
you.

But after all, the new city is not built here, for when

Carthaginian mason's mark.

we begin to dig foundations, an ox's head is found ;
and the oracle says, "This is a fruitful land, but one
full of labour, and the city would ever be servant to
others."   A little further on we try again.   This time
a horse's head turns up, and the oracle foretells, "This

shall be a powerful nation, great in war; and this

The harbour of Carthage.

foundation signifieth victory." Dido is content. A
radiant city rises as if by magic, and a temple stands

upon the hill once encompassed by the ox-hide. The
hill and its temple are called Byrsa—the hide—but the
name of the great city is Carthage. Harbours and

Carthaginian wall postern.

reservoirs, massive walls and curious posterns show
what Dido's engineers and masons can do.

Poor Dido! we thought to leave her at rest in the

city her hands have founded: queen of the fairest
daughter of hoary old Tyre. Alas! her beauty is her
undoing, for the name of it goes abroad and a barbarian
king, Iarbas, vows either to wed her or to destroy both
her and her city utterly. He sends an embassy, but
they fear to tell the rude king's message, and contrive
a scheme whereby to entrap her. "Our king," say
they, "is minded that his people be taught more gentle
manners; but who will ever be found generous enough
to teach them, for they are as beasts of the field?"
And the sweet queen answers, "No man should refuse
to sacrifice himself for others, or even give his life for
them, if need be." Then the men exult, saying,

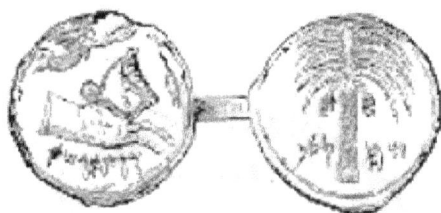

Carthaginian coin.

"According to thine own words, so be it, O queen; what
thou hast counselled for others, let thyself perform."
And Dido perceives the trick, and with bitter tears
prays the messengers first to grant her three months in
which to bewail her lost Acerbas, after which she will
fulfil the will of the gods.

But Dido cannot be false to a husband so dearly
loved. In a remote corner of the city behold a vast
pyre. Sheep and oxen, priests and people, and the
hapless queen herself are here; up to heaven rises the
smoke of a great sacrifice. The frantic people shout
and scream, "Go to your husband! Go to Iarbas!"
And Dido, stern and pale, and clothed in white from
head to foot, stretches out her hand and takes a sword

from a soldier at her elbow, and stands upon the pyre
in the midst of the multitude. A sudden hush falls on
man and beast; Queen Dido gazes for a moment on
the surging crowd, then rings out her last message to
the men of Carthage:—" Ye bid me go to my husband.
It shall be as you desire, for see, before your very eyes
I go!" There is a swift, uplifted arm, a flash of steel
in the afternoon sun—and Dido is gone to Acerbas.

Yes, Dido is dead; but Carthage—queen of the
Internal Sea—lives on, and there is no more prosperous
nation under heaven than this youngest-born of the
Region of Palm.

CHAPTER VII.

PLAINS OF WILD ALMOND

THROUGH the flower-laden fields of Araby we reach the mysterious dwellings of the "pure men" of Iran. Temples of fire, flanked by "towers of silence;" valleys of jewels; gardens of lilies; these are before you, behind you, and round about you. You are on a high table-land with the sea 4000 feet below. On all sides

Fire-temple of Zoroaster.

the mountains keep solemn watch over countless altars, from which the curling smoke rises more and more thickly, as the eternal fires are fanned by the priests of Zoroaster. The air is heavy with the scent of roses from the vale of Cashmere, and white with scattered blossoms of the wild almond. Would you descend from your lofty station? you must beware the southward passes, for there is no gentle slope on *that* side, only three gigantic steps from summit to base; but the

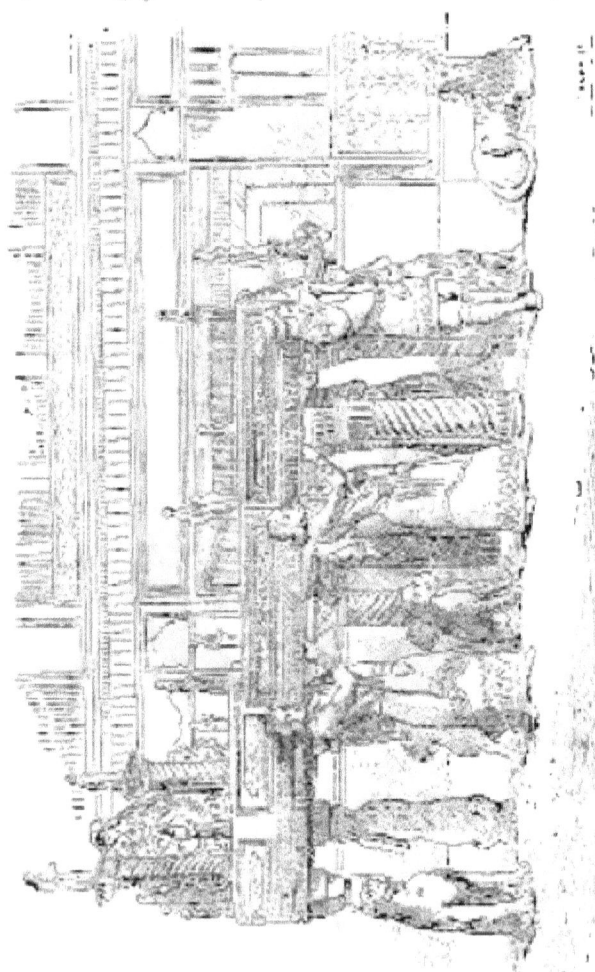

Throne of the Shah.

other sides are more pleasant to tread, covered with delicate green grass and starred all over with blood-red

P

poppies, like rubies set in a belt of emerald. By your leave we will stay where we are however, for from our present coign of vantage we can overlook nearly all the cities of Iran and observe the people at their daily avocations.

Mirror Pavilion at Ispahan.

You are in the streets of Ispahan—sleepy Ispahan, where they are too lazy to get out of your way if you happen to fall over a prostrate figure or two in your peregrinations. Its Mirror Pavilion is still a wonder to see, and once there was a wonderful tower here, 150

Shrine of Imam Hossain at Kerbela.

F 2

Palace at Shiraz.

feet high, and built of the bones of all kinds of animals,
the victims of Shah Abbas in one single day's sport.
But the glory of Ispahan is departed and her monuments are forgotten. Northward lies Teheran; on
the west Kerbela, city of a thousand shrines; and away
to the south you see royal Persepolis with, close by,

Ruins of the Palace at Susa.

the world-renowned gardens of Shiraz. Here, say the
sons of Iran, was the Garden of Eden—you see
everybody who has the ghost of a claim appropriates
that delectable spot! Here, by the same token, were
created Adam and Eve, and here also Noah, Zoroaster
and Darius first opened their infant eyes. Susa too

is in sight, once the pride of all Iran, and the summer
residence of her kings.

But the town seems waking up, and just a suspicion
of excitement is creeping over the place. Something

A family party.

is in the wind you may be sure, for a Persian never
excites himself about nothing. In another minute a
cloud of dust appears in the horizon, reminding you,
for all the world, of the opportune arrival—in a similar
cloud—of the two brothers of the unlucky Fatima,

when that lady was about to suffer the punishment
due to inquisitive wives. Instead of the two fiery
horsemen, however, a train of camels, heralded by a
jolly-looking family party on a mule, crosses the plain
and slowly threads its way up the steep incline to the
plateau of Persia. It is the great caravan from Bagdad,
and is going to Kelát.
Some portion of its mer-
chandise is sure to find a
purchaser in the san-
guinary Khan of the
latter district, but there
can be no objection to
driving a bargain by the
way, and moreover there
are goods to be bought
here which will be vastly
appreciated, and yield a
substantial interest at
both ends of the journey.
Ispahan pottery and
Kashan copper-work find
a market anywhere. So
the travellers halt; the
camels are unloaded, and
the wares placed on view.
There is a perfect din of
voices by this time;
everybody has something
to sell, and nearly everybody has his eye on

Mir Khodadad, Khan of
Kelát.

something which he intends to buy, if by good luck he
can beat the greedy owner down low enough. His
private figure is about half, and his opening offer not a
quarter the sum asked for the article, but he will carry
the latter off for all that, and at his own price too.
All this bickering and bully-ragging takes time how-

Pottery of Ispahan.

Chateau in Forest.

ever, and you and I have something else to do than
waste an afternoon in haggling over twopence, when

A wayside inn between Teheran and Ispahan.

A Persian nomad dwelling.

ten minutes' square dealing would settle the business.
Leave the bargain-hunters to their devices then, I

beseech you; a stroll through Ispahan will be quite as entertaining!

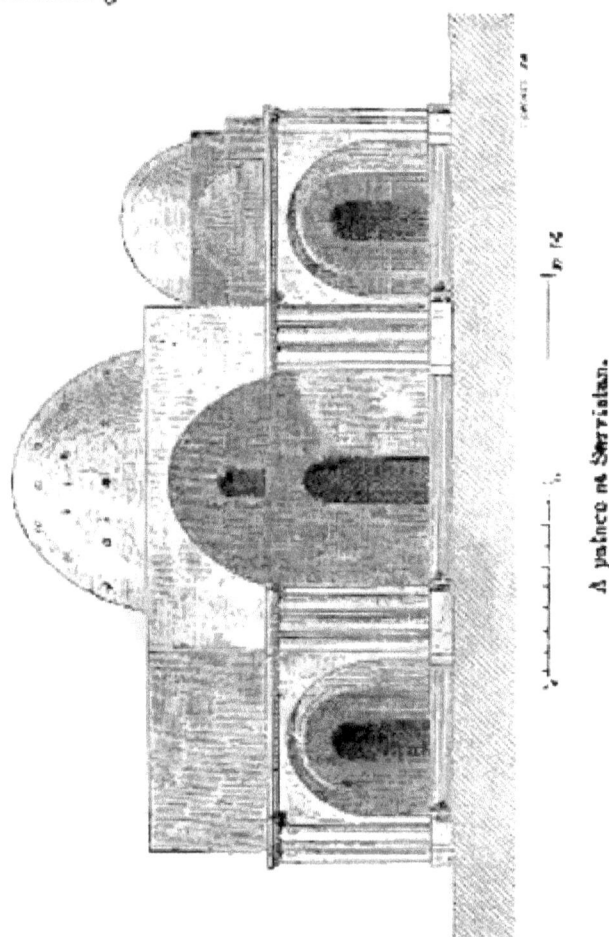

A palace at Serristan.

Persian habitations run to extremes. The average house is barn-like in its simplicity, while mud-huts and ramshackle tents provide shelter for the less particular

section of the community. Cheek by jowl with these
come palaces, dwellings most splendid to look upon—
outside!   Inside—well, there is sometimes much *savoi*

Interior of the Sarvistan palace.

decoration, but a lack of furniture which fits badly
with our ideas of comfort. The plenishing of a Persian
house is pretty nearly expressed by the one word

"carpets." On these the people deposit themselves,
bend their knees under them, and sit on their heels;

Here we are at the house of my good friend Ali
Hassein, one of the cleverest metal-workers in Ispahan.

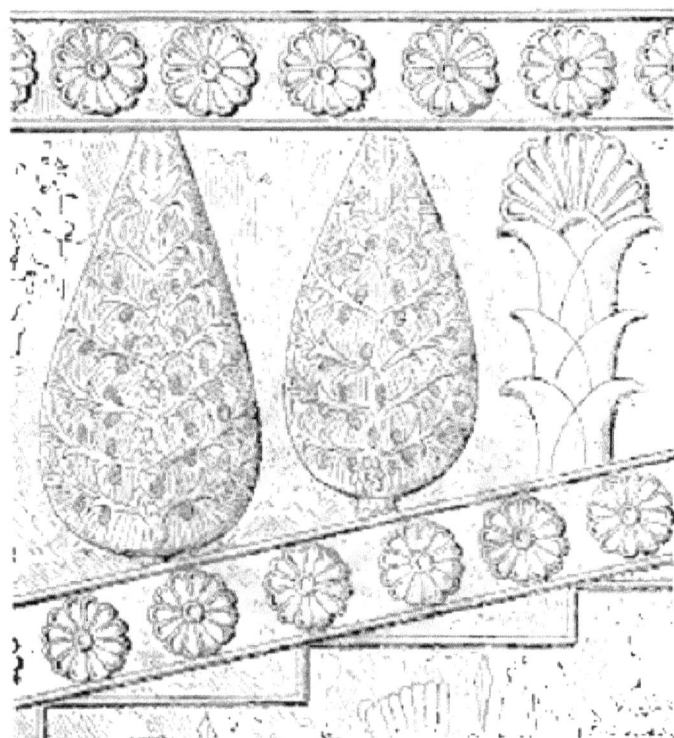

Persian wall decoration.

Did I tell you that besides pottery, Ispahan is famous
for its brass and steel work? No! Very stupid
of me; why, the damascening here is the finest in the
world. But I have a little affair to settle with old
Hassein, and you can come and look over his goods

while I arrange my business. Ah, he is damascening at this very moment, so you will see the process. The true damascene is made of a special kind of iron; and this, after forging, lies for about a week in a bath heated with cow's dung, which is believed to contain the salts necessary for forming the finest damascene. Every care is taken to keep the heat steady, but not too intense, and objects are allowed to keep the same temper with which they leave the bath. Then follows

The metal-workers' house.

much polishing, and now my friend dissolves three parts of a certain mineral—Sal ammoniac, I should say —in ten parts of water, over a slow fire, and goes on to finish his work. Just watch how he warms the lamp-stand he is holding, and then "dabs" it all over with a cotton wad dipped in the liquor over the fire. That is to bring out the fibre of the metal, and if the damascene does not show sufficiently, the whole process will be gone over again. It appears to be satisfactory; so the artizan proceeds to ornament it with gold and

Damascened lamp-stand.   A hookah. (Engraved brass.)

silver. He cuts out fine channels, following the pattern chosen, and into these he lays gold and silver wire, hammers them level, and gives the whole surface a grand final polish. Sometimes only gold leaf, rubbed in and burnished with agate, is used in the decoration; but this is never so lasting as the wire. The copper-smiths of Kashan turn out very similar work to that at Ispahan; they often coat their wares with white metal before applying the ornamentation however. Here is a ewer treated in this way: it has a long spout and hinged lid, and is usually full of rose-water ready to be poured over your hands by an attendant, should you so desire. The beautiful "Dakhl-i-pul" next to it is of engraved brass, with perforated cover and swing handles. It is just about to be sent off to the roast-meat shop opposite, where it will be suspended for the customers to drop their coppers into. What a pro-fanation!

One other industry of Ispahan I must show you, so make your adieux to old Hassein and step with me over to the women's quarter. On the way there are a few calls to make. Kazi Imád-ed-Din Kazvini used to say, "The weavers of Ispahan make cotton veils four cubits square which weigh but four miscals (half an ounce)," and the gold and silver brocade made here is so beautiful that a petticoat of it is considered cheap at £20, even in Persia. Yonder is a batch of calico-printers; I daresay you didn't know it before, but in all probability block-printing was invented in Persia. Instead of a dotted or repeating pattern, the cloth—which is in quite short lengths—is covered with one design. After being cut into convenient pieces, the calico is immersed in a dung bath, washed, dried, and laid in a second bath—of pounded gall-nuts this time —till thoroughly impregnated, then dried again in the sun, and is ready to print.

The design is divided into compartments, a separate

Copper ewer from Kashan.

Q

Metal vase " Dabbl-o-pul."

block being used, not only for each compartment, but
for each colour in these. Black and red, the basis
colours, are first applied. Black is made by placing
any old nails or scraps of rusty iron that come handy
into water for a fortnight. After withdrawing the nails,
and adding castor oil and alum, the water is boiled to
a consistency suitable for the printer. Red is obtained
from a mixture of alum and Bol Armenian, with a
muslin bagful of the gum of the apricot-tree thrown in.
Black and red applied, the calico is boiled in madder
and gall-nuts for five hours and laid in the sun for a
month to bleach and "set." Next comes the blue, made
of indigo beaten to a paste and boiled with lime, potash
and grape treacle. Browns and yellows—from pomegranate skins boiled in alum—follow the blue, and
other colours after that again, the finishing touches
being painted in by hand. After every application the
cotton is washed and dried. I have always wondered
why no amount of soap, soda, or sun seemed to affect
the colours in my Bagdad draperies. After to-day I
would be equally surprised to find any invention of
man that could move them!

Next door to the calico-printer's stands the carpet
factory; for the matter of that, there is one on each
side. Real Persian carpets! How often you have
admired them; but you never expected to see one
made. Nothing could be more primitive that the
"plant." There is not a vestige of machinery in the
place, nothing but the clever fingers of these two
women. Their loom is only a rude frame on which to
stretch the warp, and the woof is formed of short
woollen threads twisted and knotted by hand into the
warp, without even a shuttle.

They have just come to the end of a row, and as one
inserts a wooden comb into the warp, the other hammers
it down against the new row of woof, which is thus
pressed tightly into the rest of the web. When all

the weaving is done, they will cut the woof even to
form the pile. It is a slow and wearisome process, but
the result is very lovely, and £4 a yard will gladly be
given by some western grandee for the hand-made
carpet of these two Kurd women.

In the last house in the row sits a girl making a
carpet of quite another kind. She has a lapful of
scraps of variously-coloured cloth, and is sewing them
into a fanciful patchwork, working over the seams with
many beautiful needlework stitches. You look per-
plexed; where have you seen just such work as this?

Persian carpet weavers.

"Crazy patchwork!" you exclaim. Perfectly correct,
my friend, you've hit it; "Crazy" patchwork! and
made in Ispahan centuries before ever yours was
dreamt of! There is nothing new under the sun, you
see; and I rather fancy the work of the little Persian
maid there takes the shine out of any you could show.
There is at any rate a method in her madness which is
too often absent in your patchwork! Turn the corner
now, will you, and here we are among the chattering
traders again. Things are tolerably quiet, and there
is a smirk of satisfaction on every face: every man
Jack flatters himself he has outdone his neighbour!

Persian rug in cloth patchwork.

The excitement is not to subside quite yet however; a second cavalcade appears on the brow of the hill, and a score of necks are craned to take stock of the new arrival. One glance is enough; every son of Iran takes to his heels, and you and I are left sole spectators of the scene. Mules are the beasts of burden this time, and each is loaded with a couple of pairs of long, narrow packages, tightly tied up in blue canvas bags.

A corpse caravan.

They are slung across, and dangle on each side of the animals in a most uncomfortable manner, bumping first against the ribs of the patient steeds, and then against their nearest neighbours on either hand with such thuds as would convince you that they don't contain anything either valuable or breakable. "Cotton bales," did you say? Not a bit of it; this, my simple friend, is a corpse caravan! Before it has approached much nearer, you will have realized that for yourself, for it has been ten days on its journey, and between

the bumping and the burning sun, there is some reason
to believe that the sooner the long packs arrive at their
destination the better will it be for all who have to do
with them! They have come from a distant corner of
Persia, and are bound for the sacred city of Koom,
where it is the ambition of a certain class of the people
to be buried.

The people of Iran, as all the world knows, revere

Graven image of Ahura-Mazdh.

the sun and fire above all created things; but I take
up the cudgels against those who set them down as
fire-worshippers. Strictly speaking, they are nothing
of the sort, and though many errors and absurdities
have crept into their religion since Zoroaster passed
into the "city of the silent," it still teaches that the
sun and the fire are but emblems of the great God who
created both. The primitive religion was polytheism.
They worshipped the sun, moon, and the whole host of

heaven ; but Zoroaster preached a simpler faith—a pantheon of two—Ahûra-Mazda, the "good spirit" who strives continually for the welfare of man, and Angrô-Mainzûs, the "evil one," who for ever assails him.

"The light of God is concealed under all that shines," says the Avesta, Zoroaster's sacred book ; and as perfect purity in body and mind is the one thing needful to a Zoroastrian's salvation, the pure elements, the air he breathes, the water he drinks, and the earth he treads, must be kept from every unclean influence. But above all, most that purest element, fire, be

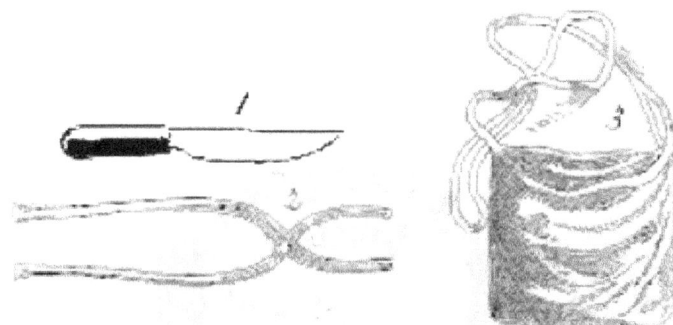

Sacrificial utensils of the Parsees.
1. **Haoma-knife.**   2. **Tongs** to trim the sacred fire.   8. The "Paitidâna" or mouth-cloth worn in presence of the sacred fire.

guarded from contamination. Not even the breath of the "pure men" must sully it, and it is with covered lips that they approach to perform their sacred office before it. They are simple and devout men, these priests of fire ; always patient, satisfied with a little bread, or whatever is offered them to eat, and studying, according to the light that is in them, to preserve purity and truth among their people. Haoma is their sacred plant, and a priestly outfit consists of a knife, wherewith to cut the Haoma ; a cup in which to offer

libations of the juice when extracted; a bundle of rods
and tongs with which to stir the sacred fire, perform
charms, and when necessary, to kill impure animals;
and finally the Paitidâna, or mouth veil. Purity is not
the only virtue enjoined by Zoroaster. From their
youth up, Parsi children are instructed in truthfulness,
industry, the cultivation of trees, and the rearing of
dogs. Here are some texts from the Avesta:—"Lying
and borrowing go hand in hand, for the borrower seeks
day and night to deceive the creditor." . . . "Long
sleep, O man, is not good : he who rises first will come
into Paradise." . . . "He who plants trees, who gives
water to the thirsty earth and takes it away when too
abundant, he honours the earth; but to him who tills
her not she says, 'Thou wilt go to the doors of others and
beg for bread; in idleness thou wilt ask for bread and
get but little.'" You are not surprised after this to see
how carefully every tree is tended in Iran, and only in
the upbringing of children are dogs put in the background. "Protect dogs for six months—children for
seven years," says the Avesta.

An old Zoroastrian once wove me a whole garland of
Persian romances, and among them was the story of
the origin of so-called fire-worship. Shall I tell it
to you?

"King Hooshung, of ancient memory, passing one
day by a lofty mountain with his attendants, beheld a
vast black object, whose two eyes were as fountains of
blood, and the smoke from its nostrils obscured the
whole heavens. It was a monstrous serpent, glossy
and hideous, and Hooshung was wise, and regarded it
from a safe distance, then assailed it with stones and
the vigour of a hero. The creature vanished for ever,
but the stones smote the rock and split it, and a great
flame blazed forth. Thus a stone became the producer
of fire, and Hooshung said, 'This fire is from God, let
us bow before it.' And when night came, the whole

mountain was covered with flames, and the king and all his servants prostrated themselves, and they became the worshippers of God in the fire!"

I believe there is something in the air of Persia that compels story-telling! What tales were ever so en-

The huntsmen of Iran.

trancing as those told on the thousand and one nights by that clever Sultana Schoheruzade? I only know of another such galaxy, and that is contained in the book of the "Thousand and one *Days*."[1] Perhaps you never

---

[1] Justin McCarthy.

before heard of such a book !   In that case I recommend
you to read it without loss of time, and in the meantime
I am so smitten with the story-telling mania that I
really must give you another of my old Parsi's legends.

In ancient times there lived a king of Persia, named
Baharam, whose ruling passion was the chase, and one
fine day he set out to hunt accompanied by a lady
whom he loved, and a score of courtiers.   After per-
forming unheard-of feats, he shot an arrow so as just
to graze the ear of a sleeping antelope.   The animal
looked up and raised its hoof to flick off what it sup-
posed to be a fly : at that instant Baharam, with a
second arrow, fixed hoof and ear together !   A shout
of admiration burst from every throat, save that of
the lady, and the king turned to her with surprise.
" Practice makes perfect," she coolly remarked, and
evinced no further interest in the matter.   Without
further ado the irate monarch banished her from the
kingdom.   For a long time she dwelt in the upper
room of a distant castle, but it was very lonely, and for
company the poor soul bought a newly-born calf and
carried it up and down stairs with her every day.

Four years afterwards, Baharam chanced to pass
that way and stop to refresh himself.   What was his
amazement to see a young woman carrying a full-grown
cow up a flight of twenty stairs.   Such an out of the
way proceeding tickled his fancy prodigiously, and he
demanded an instant explanation.   The lady returned
answer that only if the king would come to her apartment unattended, would she reveal her secret.
Curiosity got the better of him, and for once Baharam
did as he was bid.

On reaching the chamber he launched out with
extravagant praises, but was promptly told not to
bestow praise where it was not deserved ; " Practice
makes perfect," added the dame, looking slyly from
under her yashmak.   The king recognized his lady-

love, and had the common sense to profit by the lesson. The lady was reinstated, and it is to be hoped her influence was as lasting as it was salutary.

I am not sure whether you will agree that the wife of the great king Jamshíd did him an equally good turn when she invented wine : rather a doubtful benefit for such a peppery race, you may think! It was quite accidental, like many another invention that has made a noise in the world. The king was excessively fond of grapes, and in order to have them all the year round he, on one occasion, packed a quantity into vessels and stored them in a vault. Alas! when opened, they were found fermented and sour as vinegar. Nothing doubting, Jamshíd sealed them up again, and labelled them " Poison " till such time as the horrible concoction could be got rid of. Now the queen was a martyr to neuralgic headaches; and one night, mad with pain, and longing only for death, she remembered the " Poison " in the cellar. Down she ran, helped herself liberally, and composed herself to die. In the morning she awoke—another woman. It was just the medicine she needed, and whenever the trouble returned a dose was sure to set her right again. But at last the " Poison " was finished ; her majesty had to confess her misdeeds to Jamshíd, and explain the effects of the grape juice. I don't know what he said to her, but more wine was at once made ; both king and court were charmed with the new beverage, and in Persia it is called Zeher-e-khoosh, " delightful poison," to this day !

You begin to think there is a tale tacked to everything here ; well, you are not far wrong, for Persia is a veritable garden of romance, and as I hinted before, the story-telling mania is most infectious. However, we will turn over a new leaf and look for something more serious than romances.

You have only just pulled me up in time ; I had all

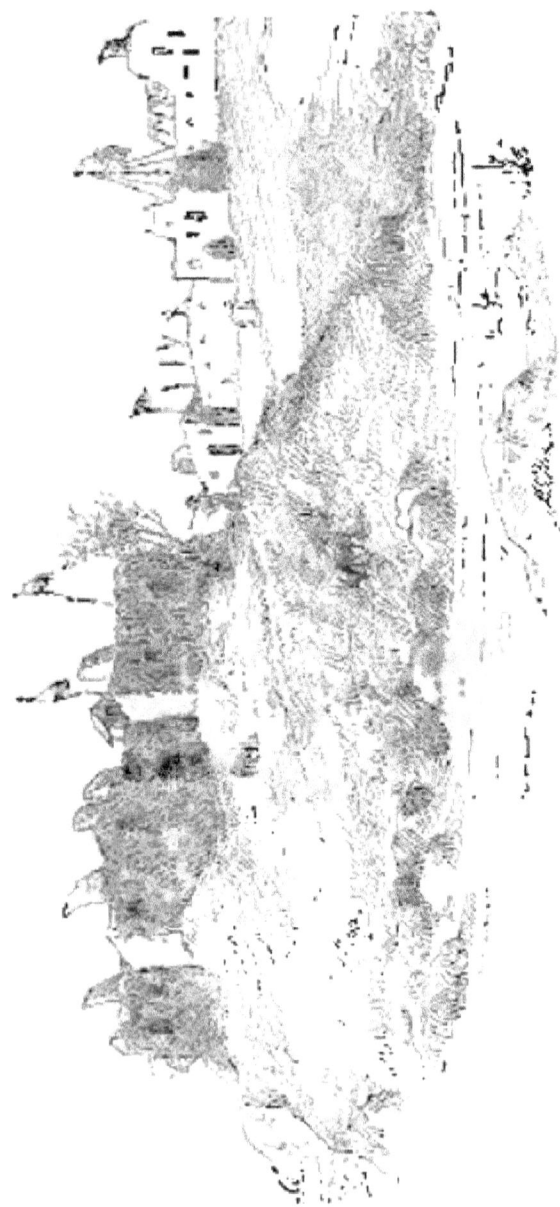

The land of the fire-worshippers.

but forgotten that to-day is the feast of "Neuraz," and we must on no account miss that. Yonder is the enclosure which serves as a temple. As you draw nearer you see the hole in the ground from which issues the pale blue flame of the quenchless fire. The night has been spent by the "pure men" in silence, and ever since daybreak one of them has watched with veiled lips beside this symbol of eternal purity. At his side are two altars on which the faithful will lay their offerings. Come closer: let us follow in the wake of this band of priests. Clad in white raiment, girt about with golden girdles, and with hair floating over their shoulders, they are the very personification of all that is noble and pure. But hark! there is the low chant of the servants of the high-priest. The congregation listens for an instant with one foot uplifted, one hand on lip and nostril, then falls on the ground before the holy man. The latter moves slowly to the centre of the temple, clothed in white wool, with belt of wrought silver, bearing in one hand the sacred rods and in the other the Avesta. He prostrates himself in silent prayer, then waving his hand as if tracing a huge circle, he calls in a loud voice:—

"Souls belonging to God! forget your earthly covering, raise your spirit pure to your creator and say, 'Oh thou! without beginning or end, we adore, we supplicate thee. Grant us strength to suffer without murmuring the trials thou hast allotted us. . . . It was on this day that holy Zoroaster came to teach us regarding those gifts with which thou hast blest us. . . . We present offerings then with humility, and pray that when the day comes that the sacred element shall run over the earth, doing the will of divine anger, it may spare the pure, but have no mercy on the wicked.'"

The holy man now covers his mouth, and stirring the fire with the sacred rods, casts into it his own offering; then sits down till every worshipper has passed before him and thrown in his gift of amber, gold, or spices.

This ends the usual service of the Guebers,[1] but to-day being the Neuruz, all who have committed offences are waiting to implore the intercession of the " pure men " on their behalf. That which is dead—be it the body, or anything parted from the body—belongs to the spirit of darkness, and brings impurity on all who touch it. " Carry away then," saith Ahûra-Mazda, " all cut nails and hair, twenty paces from the pure fire ; dig a hole, and praying nine times, bury them there ; so shall they become weapons *against* instead of *for* the spirits of evil."

Slight pollution is removed by washing with water ; uttering the while certain imprecations against the deavas.[2] But here comes a criminal of the deepest dye ; one whose guilt can only be cleansed by the severest measures. He has slain a water-dog ! the friend and protector of another man's goods, and he is worthy of death. The good priest would save his life, however, and seeing that the man has come to his senses, he imposes a penance which will stand instead of the extreme penalty. Shamefaced and penitent, the culprit hears the sentence read against him. For the undoing of a common dog 2000 stripes would have sufficed, but for the life of the pure water-dog, 10,000 are not too many. Moreover, if he would save his soul, he must give 10,000 parcels of wood, hewn and dry, to the sacred fires ; he must kill 10,000 snakes, and a like number of tortoises, lizards, ants, flies, and rats, all impure animals ; he must fill up 10,000 impure holes in the earth ; give to the temple a set of vessels for holy rites ; to a warrior a suit of armour ; to a husbandman an outfit of implements, a house and a piece of land. Then must he give to the priests

---

[1] Giaours, or followers of Zoroaster.   [2] Evil spirits.

fourteen head of cattle; build fourteen bridges over

The altars of Iron.

running water; rear fourteen young dogs; cleanse
eighteen dogs from fleas; make eighteen dry bones into

Pierced and chased incense burner.

nourishing food, and satisfy eighteen pure men with
wine and flesh. Should he fail in any one of these
expiations, he will be promptly despatched to the realms
of the "Fiend of Death," there to offer sacrifice for
ever amid the fire that burns. Poor wretch! fancy

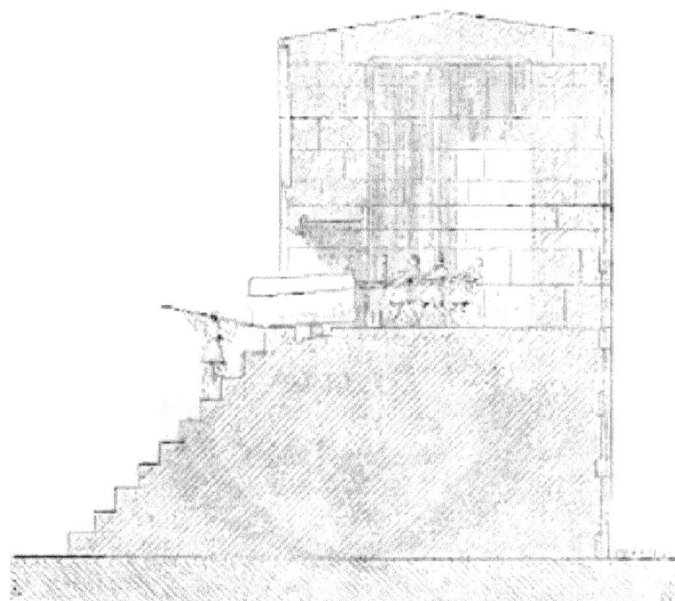

Bearing the dead to the "Tower of Silence."

trying to look grateful for a respite at such a
price?
   On another, but lesser sinner, the "Great Purifica-
tion" of the nine nights is imposed. See! they are
just about to begin. Here is the specially selected
enclosure, ninety feet distant from the fire, water, and

sacred rods.   In the midst nine pits are dug, and
round these twelve furrows drawn.   Forth comes the
priest leading the unclean, whom he first sprinkles with
the excrement of animals, and afterwards rubs over
with earth fifteen times.   At each of the nine pits the
culprit then washes three times, and the priest concludes
by fumigating him with fragrant wood, singing at the
same time many praises to Ahúra-Mazda.   For nine

Ancient "Dakhma," or Tower of Silence, near Teheran.

nights this performance is repeated, and the unclean
at last becomes clean—that is, always supposing he
does not forget to present the priest with a suitable
reward.   Failing this, the impure spirit comes again
for evermore into the niggardly man !

Nothing is so impure as a corpse ; so when a man or
a dog—the latter is quite on an equality with the
former—falls ill, there is a terrible to-do.   Three

different physicians are called in; the first, usually a priest, confines himself to charms and prayers; the second has a favourite potion which he administers to all and sundry—fever, cholera, measles, and mange

The Takht-i-Soleiman.

are all alike to him; the third, the barber very often, exercises his surgical skill in a most radical manner. Wounded limbs are simply hacked off with a chopper— bruised fingers with a razor, and the bleeding stumps in each case are dipped into boiling oil or pitch. But in

spite of the best of doctors, people *will*, and *do* die.
Now to place a corpse in water, to bury, or to burn it
is a crime too great for expiation, and to get out of the
difficulty the ingenious Parsi has invented a system of
burial which has no equal for originality. In Egypt
all the difficulty was in getting low enough; here, *au
contraire*, the one aim and object, is to get high
enough. A "tower of silence" is built on an eminence
from which the birds of prey can easily see it. Over
the top is an iron grating, and here the dead is laid,
naked, and with face upturned to the sun. Nothing

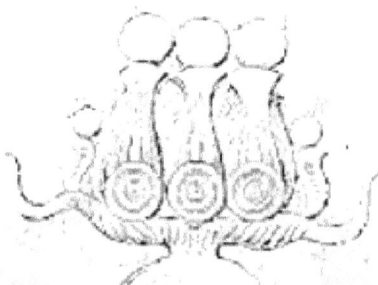

Head-dress of Cyrus.

but the sobs of the bereaved breaks the awful silence
as the body is thus given over to the dogs, the vultures,
and the elements; and only when the bones are picked
clean, and disappear through the grating into the
cavern beneath, is the dead made pure, and the annihilation of death complete.

Now for a glance at Persepolis. On the way there
we pass Istakhr, with the harem of Jamshid. West-
ward, among the gloomy depths of the mountains, are
the rock tombs of Darius and three other kings of
Iran, and you will see, right in the face of the rock,
the far-famed "drawings" of Rustem, Persia's dearest
hero. There is moreover, not very far away, the

famous Takht-i-Soleiman, or throne of Solomon.
After what you know of Zoroastrian burial, you do
not expect to find many tombs in Persia; sure enough,
it is only those of kings that have been suffered to

Enamelled slab from Cyrus' palace at Susa.

stand, and like the rock-cut tombs of Lycia, they are
simple copies of built houses.

We have reached Persepolis.

There are the "Forty columns;" the "Throne of
Jamshid," the "House of Darius;" and as we stand

Staircase of the palace of Darius.

The palace of Darius.

within the pillared halls—so like to those at Karnak—
the spirits of the dead rise up to greet us; they live
and move and have their being; they eat and drink
and laugh as in a long by-gone day; let us make
haste to welcome them, lest they, finding no human
interest in all the upper earth, depart again to the
great shadowland.

It is the court of Darius. Not so very long ago the
court was held at Susa, that was in Cyrus' time; and
you may still see the great audience-chamber there,
supported by thirty-six pillars, tall and slight, with
their capitals of kneeling horses. Cyrus, as you very
well know, made Phœnicia and Lydia, and all the
"Region of Palm" his vassals. He put his heel on the
neck of even proud Babylon, and cities that had staked
their very existence rather than submit to great
Nebuchadnezzar, opened their gates to Cyrus of Persia.
But Darius is a man of greater genius than Cyrus:
a man of gigantic intellect and born to command. He
knows not only how to conquer nations, but how to
govern them well. His wealth is beyond all computa-
tion, but something corresponding to not less than
27,000,000 sterling, is said to come into his coffers
every year. He is moreover a man of fancies, and
having the wherewithal to gratify these, he has built
him a new palace on a terrace formed by a spur of the
mountains at Persepolis. It is a perfect citadel, surrounded by three walls; the inner one sixteen cubits
high, and fortified with turrets; the second twice as
high; and the outer one square, sixty cubits high, with
on every side a colossal gate of brass. There are 200
broad steps of marble, on which ten horsemen can ride
abreast; fifteen to thirty of these steps being hewn out
of one block. Just within the gate-post is a picture of
the king, in a garment reaching to his feet, wide
sleeves, high shoes, and a tiara. From here you have
a fine view of the tomb the pious monarch has prepared

The tomb of Darius.

for the day of his dissolution. It is of white marble,

Part of a Persian throne.

seventy feet high ; the lower part plain, and forming

a basis for four rock-cut pillars, with capitals of
kneeling horses. Above the pillars rises a catafalque,
and on this, two rows of men support a beam from
which a few steps lead to the platform, on which stands
a figure of Darius before a flaming altar. In a winged
circle above floats Ahura-Mazda with the sun-disc at
his side. Still nearer you is the palace of Xerxes,

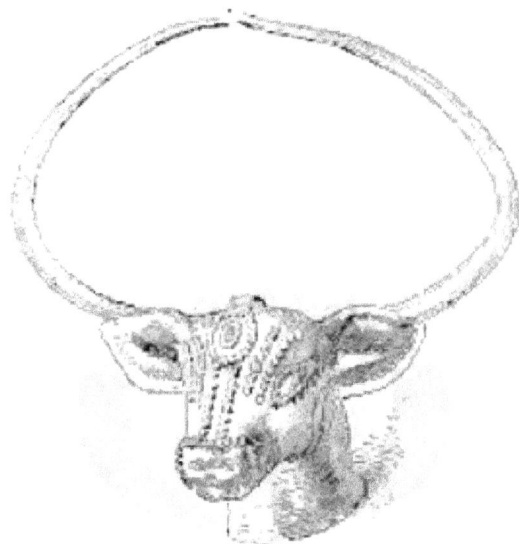

Electrum ornament.

the king's son and heir; for the young prince has
arrived at man's estate and desires to have a home of
his own.

Now we are in the royal audience chamber, the "Hall
of a hundred columns," and behold! seated on a throne
of gold, is the great Darius himself. Over his head
waves a canopy dyed with the precious purple of Tyre,
and supported by four gilded and jewelled pillars. The
Persian architect has evidently borrowed largely from

Babylon, Assyria, and Egypt; yet he is no mere

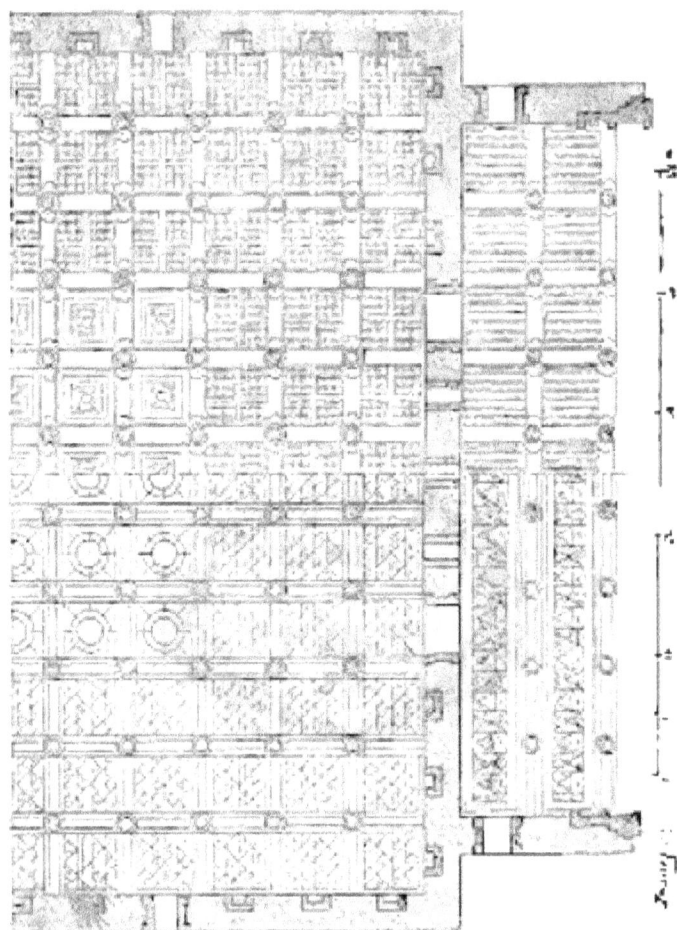

Ceiling and floor of Darius' palace.

imitator. Egyptian pillars are massive; those of Iran

the most delicate ever raised by the architects of
antiquity. Animals are portrayed with great vigour,
though they are flatter than in Assyria, and the human-
headed bulls which stand here just as at Nineveh,
have their wings more upright, and wear the Persian
tiara instead of the Assyrian cap.   Bricks are used,
but they are quite unnecessary among the plains of
Wild Almond, for there is stone in abundance; and
wood covered with gold and silver, forms no small part
of the building material.   The walls of this chamber
are entirely covered with plates of gold, and the slender
pillars which support the roof, though sixty feet high,
are but four inches in diameter.   "Floors of marble,
alabaster, pearls, and tortoise-shell," are heaped with
cushions wrought in gold, silver, and many-hued gems.
The splendid palace is filled with as splendid a court.
The king himself wears a robe of royal purple edged
with white, and embroidered with hawk and falcon, birds
of the gods, which dwell in the pure air nearest heaven
—Darius is a devout worshipper of Mazda, you see!
He has besides, purple trousers, a blue and white
tiara, and saffron-coloured shoes.   A golden girdle en-
circles his waist, and his jewels—well, they defy
description, and the nearest estimate you can make of
the value of the whole rig-out is three million sterling.

Here you see the élite of Iran, little less magnificent
than the king, yet bowing in the dust before him, and
scrupulously keeping their hands up their sleeves, to
signify that they couldn't and wouldn't use them
against him on any account.

Business is over; the royal seal has been affixed to
all documents, and the court, as usual, goes now to
banquet with the king.   Between ourselves, things
have been just scampered through anyhow, for this is
the royal birthday, the "day of perfect banquet," and
on it the king is allowed to dance, become intoxicated,
or to perform any prank which, at another time, would

get him into no end of a scrape. We may stand here

A royal staircase at Persepolis.

and watch the precession pass to the banqueting-hall;
but for any sake keep your feet off that strip of carpet!

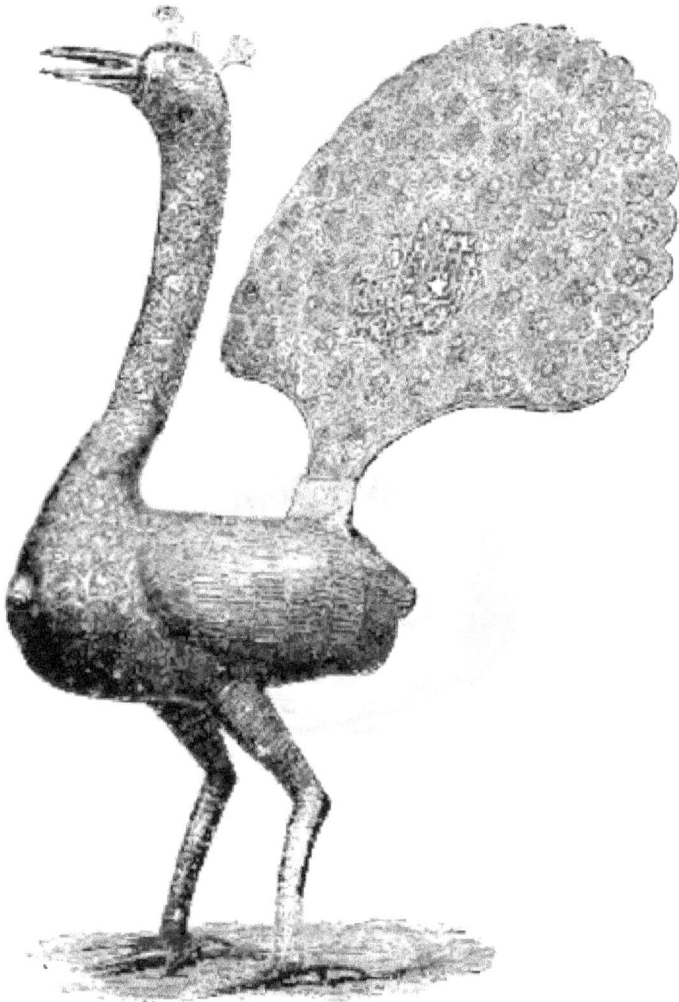

Peacock. (Engraved Brass.)

That is for Darius alone to touch. No one ever sees

the king on foot, and all along the palace courts these strips are placed for his exclusive use. Down the

grand staircase sweeps the royal cavalcade—stairs, I
must tell you, are just as much affected in Persia as
they are tabooed in Assyria—roads are cleansed and
strewn with myrtle and spices. The sacred chariot of
Mithra, drawn by eight grey horses, goes in front, next
come the priests, "pure men," bearing the sacred fire,
and after them Darius, in a chariot with six horses, his
staff-bearers walking on either side. Then follows an

Coffee-pot.   A Persian spittoon.

endless train of officers and servants;—the chamberlain;
the chief butler and his retinue ; the chief door-keeper
and his; cooks, bakers, valets, carvers, lamplighters,
spreaders of pillows and carpets, table-dressers,
ointment-makers, and sweepers-up generally.   All
these go by, as well as grooms, huntsmen, dog-keepers,
and lastly the physician-in-chief; and by the time we
reach the great hall, there isn't even standing room.
We can just see the king seated at table, with the

queen-mother above and the queen-consort below him. The nobles are seated on pillows all round—in proper order of precedence, mind you—the one most honoured and trusted being on the left, because the king can more easily defend himself with his right hand!

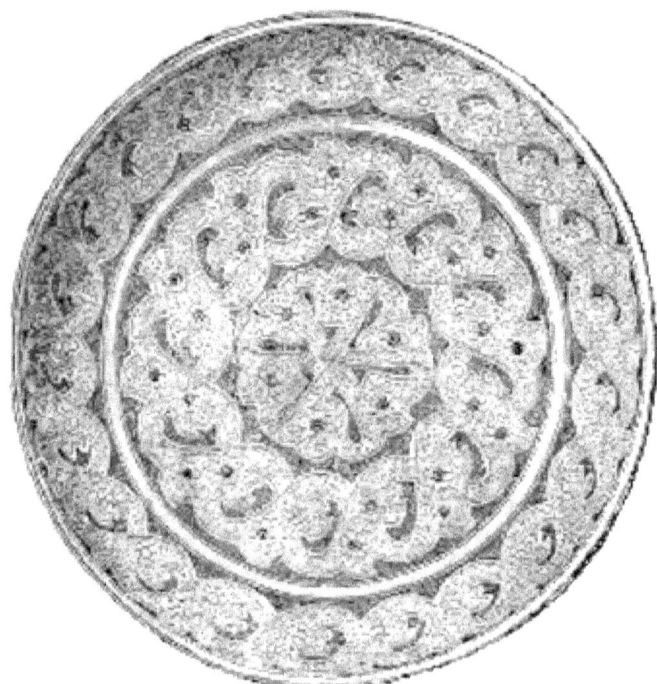

Rice dish.

The table-cloth is spread on the floor, and is of a size befitting the party. In the centre stands the great sherbet-bowl, only used on high days and holidays, from which the guests help themselves with long wooden spoons. Before each person is a flat cake which is to serve both as plate and napkin, and—don't be horrified—each rejoices in a dainty blue and white spittoon. Many kinds of food are set out, the foundation of nearly all being *chilou*, or plain boiled rice, and every dish is tasted for poison before being presented to the king. The Iranisus are great dons at preparing rice, and grow many varieties, of which the amber-scented is perhaps the favourite. But I daresay you are admiring the dishes as much as the dinner. This blue plate containing *pilao*, or rice mixed up with butter and seasonings, is a great beauty. It is from

Signet of Darius.

the famous potteries at Kashau, and is truly Persian in character. All the best pottery comes from Kashan, though Ispahan runs it very close. Indeed, so skilful are the Ispahan potters that their rivals at Yezd once sent them a challenge, a vessel weighing only one miscal (three dwt.), yet capable of holding 12 lbs. of water. The Ispahan potters sent back a vase exactly the same size and shape, weighing 12 lbs. and which could only hold one miscal of water.

These old Persians as a rule eat little and drink

less, but this is a special occasion, and there is no
telling what antics they may not be up to, so after a
brief repast the queens and their women disappear.
As there seems no likelihood of our being invited to
partake of any royal dainty, don't you think we may
as well follow suit?

At the door we turn to take a last look—and lo!
the spirits have passed into the " City of Silence," and
owls hoot in the palace of Darius.

CHAPTER VIII.

THE ISLAND OF THE ROSE APPLE.

High among the eternal snows of the Himalayas are born three rivers: the Indus, the Brahmaputra, and

Khwajah Khizr, the Indus river-god.

the Ganges.   Almost as soon as they are born, the first two leave their mysterious cradles on the northern side

of the great mountain, and steal along the valley in
opposite directions till each finds a weak place in the

Glazed tile from Scinde.

barrier; then, curling sharply round, they set to work
to widen the breaches, and, sweeping triumphantly
through into the southern plains, they enter the sea

1500 miles apart. The Ganges, on the contrary, is
southern born, and first sees the light quite close to
where the Indus emerges from the western gorge. For
a thousand miles she flows peacefully along in almost
a straight line from west to east at the feet of those
" cloud-capped towers," then she joins hands with the
Brahmaputra, and the waters of the two stately rivers
thenceforward, like Tigris and Euphrates, have one
bed and one destiny.

Thus you have a vast country, river-bound on three
sides. Now it is a three-cornered country, with its
longest point stretching far out into the ocean ; so the
sea completes the triangle which the rivers began to

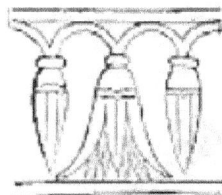

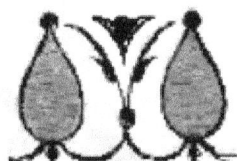

Decoration on Scindh pottery.   Decoration on Assyrian pottery.

form, and if only the Ganges had courted alliance with
the Indus as well as the Brahmaputra, the land would
have been indeed an island. It is, however, only a
peninsula, but I am inclined to humour the poetic
fancy of the people themselves, who ignore that pro-
hibitive little neck of land, and who have baptized
their beautiful home " The Island of the Rose Apple."
They sometimes also call it " Madhyama," or the
centre-land ; believing it to be the centre, not only of
all learning and art, but of the earth itself and of
all created things. And you yourself will find it hard
to tell which is the originator and which the copyist,
when you look at the exquisite art works of Hindustan,
and see how strongly they remind you of those in

Egypt and Babylon. The lotus is as familiar an object at Benares as at Thebes, so you can excuse the Hindu dogma, which says that not only Egypt, but the whole western world, borrowed the first conceptions of art and beauty from the great "Centre-land." It may be true; who knows?

Hindu Temple.

All the time we have been travelling eastwards, and stopping to fraternize with the good people along the route, these Hindus have been slowly advancing in civilization. They have reared temples and palaces of fabulous splendour, "conceived by giants and built

Sindh Pottery

by jewellers;" yet we arrive among them comparatively late in the day, only to find their habits, their beliefs, and their way of living, almost the same as they were two or three thousand years ago. They have had

Hindu cooking bowl and "long spoons."

their men of bone and men of stone—their bronze and their iron warriors, like the rest of us, and as you walk through their villages you find evidence enough that these conditions have not altogether passed away even to-day. In fact the Hindu is now a curious con-

glomeration of primitive simplicity, eastern superstition, and western refinement.   Above all things he is a
religious man; everything he does and makes has

Glazed plate from Scindh.

some sacred meaning or object, and to understand him
you must become acquainted with his gods.   Look for
example at the village potter here; very few craftsmen

are more in demand than he, and as you stand and
watch him throwing off those shapely vessels, with a
dexterity and grace most fascinating to a bystander,
you wonder whatever the villagers can want with such
a limitless supply of cooking pots and clay frying-pans.
Hour after hour he sits on the ground beside his
wheel—a horizontal fly-wheel, about three feet in
diameter, which is started by hand and then spins on
for six or seven minutes, still and steady as a sleeping
top—and the heap of clay on the centre of the wheel
is, almost by magic, transformed into jars and dishes
of most beautiful form. There seems absolutely no
end to them, but the man himself would tell you that
a really religious Hindu never uses the same earthen
vessel twice, and this accounts for the never-ending
demand for his wares, and also explains why the
baking and polishing are so meagre. In addition to
his dish-making, the potter supplies the little painted
clay idols which are thrown away every day after being
worshipped ; he also makes bricks and tiles, beats the
drum, and chants the hymns at marriages, prepares the
mutton stew for the harvest festivals, and performs
many other minor functions, so that he is a man of no
small importance in the village. His office is generally
hereditary, and he has an assured income of nearly
£12 per annum, on which he considers himself rich
indeed !

But let us look round and see what the rest of the
village is like. It is a long, irregular street made up
of a number of separate homesteads, each consisting
of about four bamboo huts. These are raised slightly
off the ground by being built on little platforms of
earth. Each hut contains but one apartment, nearly
twenty feet by ten, having low sides and an arched
roof thatched with grass, the projecting eaves forming
verandahs both back and front.

Hindu sacrificial vessels, etc.

Each homestead is placed round an open space called the home-space, where the children play and the women spin. This hut, so much better than the other three, is reserved as the sitting-room and reception-room for strangers, though very often the male members sleep here on mats on the floor. Sometimes the proprietor indulges in a charpoy, or four-legged frame, with canvas stretched across, but our present host is not well enough off for that.

On the opposite side of the quadrangle is the women's room, and next to it is the kitchen, containing the *chula* or mud fireplace; while the remaining hut is the *gola* or grain storehouse. Here in the kitchen is that indispensable utensil, the *dhenki*, an immense pestle and mortar wherewith the women are husking and pounding the rice for the children's dinner. Each group of dwellings has its own little plot on which the vegetables and plants are grown for the family curry, and whence fruit is often carried to market; and

Leg of bedstead (lacquer).

here is the tank or pond, a most valued possession, usually shared by half-a-dozen householders. Lucky

The fruit-seller.

is the man who has one all to himself, as you will realize in about five minutes if you remain where you

T

are. The wife of our worthy host has decided that
this is a suitable time to wash the clothes of the household ; her next door neighbour has unfortunately come

The village cobbler.

to a similar conclusion regarding her six children and
her entire stock of dishes, and they arrive at the tank
with their respective possessions at one and the same

moment. Ructions between the two ladies, of course; remarks more personal than polite; a plate or two broken on the one side; a kerchief in tatters on the other. Eventually, by the aid of the cobbler hard by, a compromise is arrived at; the dishes lie over for

Hindu woman in a "Burka," or Mantilla.

another day and the children are permitted to fish though not to wash. The laundry-woman settles down comfortably to her work, and the defeated one consoles herself with the reflection that, at any rate, the larder will be all the fuller when the children come home.

This would be equally the case if she had left them at the gutter instead of the pond, for in India, every little pool and ditch, though dry for months, literally swarms with fish at the first downpour of rain. In spite of occasional skirmishes of the nature of the tank scene,

Primitive silver Hindu jewellery.

the Hindu female is a most amiable and peaceable creature, and for gentle womanliness might well serve as a pattern to her more cultured western sisters. She is unspoilt by the artificiality which makes the European belle so unattractive, and she neither knows nor cares one jot or tittle for that heart-burning question— woman's rights.

What a miserable attempt at a straight line a Hindu does make! Just look at the rows of paddy behind the village: they are enough to make the methodical Assyrian come out of his dish-cover coffin and offer to level things up a little. Fences and furrows, one is as bad as the other, and it is lucky that encroachments are not seriously regarded, for partitions a yard or two

Native gold jewellery of Bombay.

out of the straight are small matters in this part of the world.

Now we are approaching the finest house in the hamlet. It is the jeweller's, as you may easily know by the throng of maidens standing round, each with a piece of money in her hand, and waiting her turn to explain what manner of ornament she wants made from it. By-and-by she becomes the delighted possessor of an exquisite bit of gold or silver decoration,

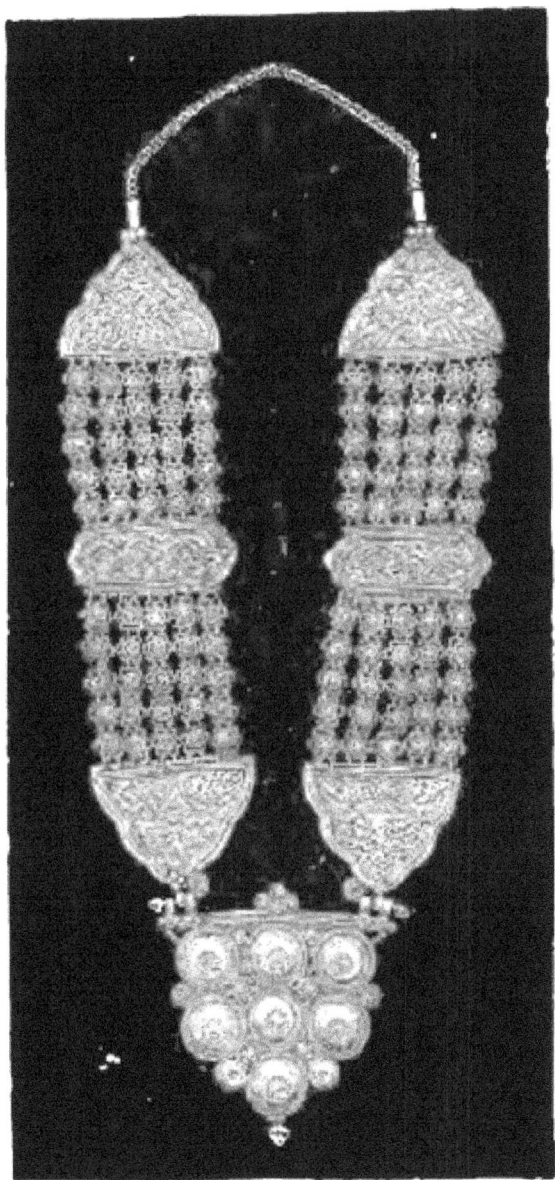

Silver necklace

equally lovely in design and workmanship. Here are some of the prettiest things in the shop: pretty enough to satisfy the most exacting of these dusky beauties. This jewelled comb almost baffles description. The foundation is a sort of leaf-scroll of emerald and green enamel on pure gold, and there are rows upon rows of matchless pearls and brilliants; but I think you will admit that yonder magnificent shrine-screen of pierced and hammered silver is a peerless

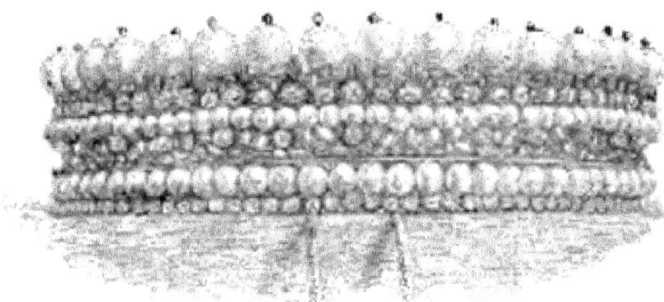

Pearl and diamond hair comb.

example of the craftsman's skill, and puts all the ladies' jimcracks into the shade.

Next door lives a marvellous worker in enamels; there is simply no one to compare with him in all the world. Can anything be more gorgeous than the inkstand he is now busy with? It is shaped like an Indian gondola, but is formed of a jewelled peacock, whose tail, sweeping under the boat, is a perfect blaze of enamel; and the canopy of the inkbottle is of green, blue, and ruby transparent enamels laid over gold. The wood and ivory carving, the lacquer-work and the metal-ware which you see in the various stages of completion in adjoining workshops attract you nearly

Pierced silver shrine-screen, Madras.

as much as the jewellery, but for the present we must
pass them by, for there is another call of even greater

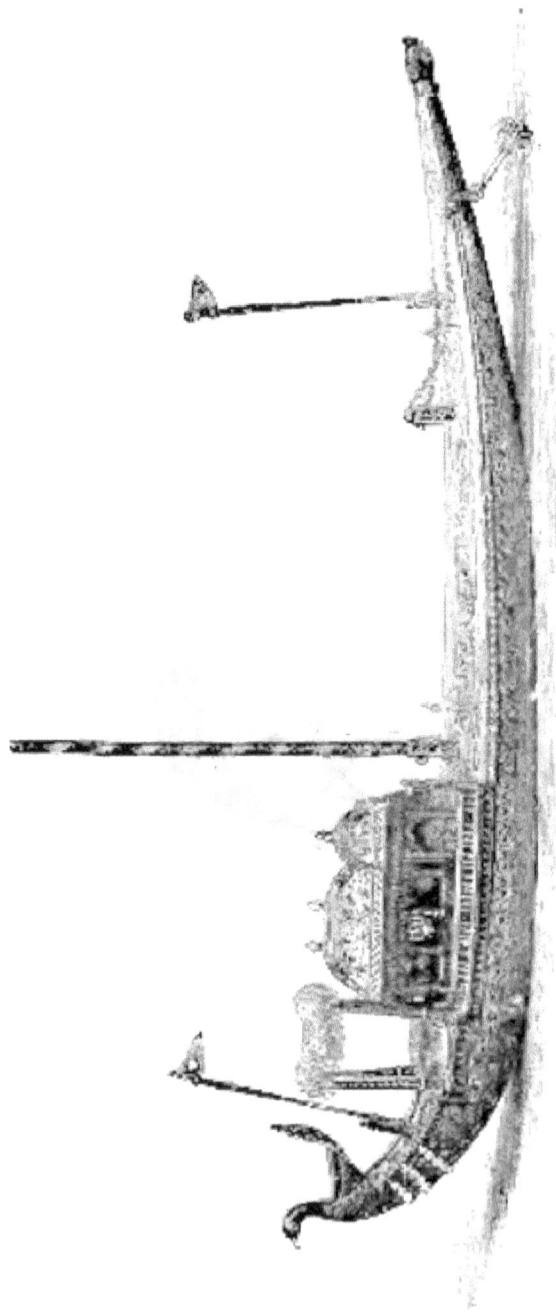

Inboard in spdd and orqczne.

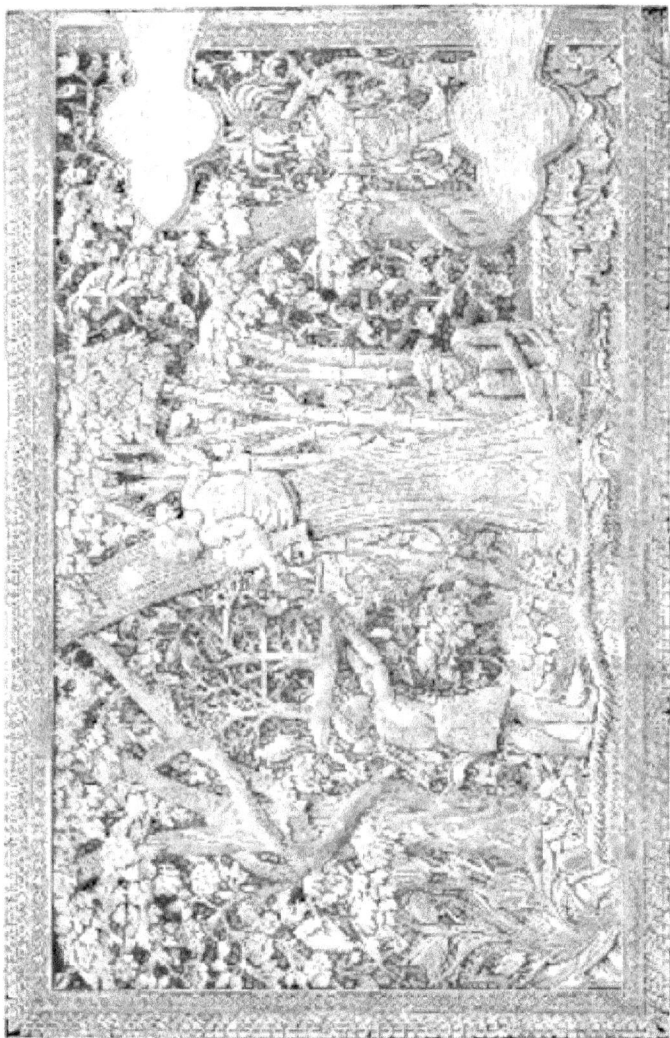

Elaborately carved sandalwood.

importance we must not omit to pay. The school-

Carved ivory comb, Bombay.

master would be mightily indignant if we overlooked *him*, so we will follow the children of our friend the silversmith, who are just setting off for school. Each of the older ones carries under his arm a bundle of neatly-cut palm-leaves on which to write; behind his ear is a reed pen, and he carries an earthen colour-pot in his hand, together with a little fried rice for his lunch. The road is long and dusty, but there is plenty to amuse you as you trudge on. The children in front make you open your eyes as you see them each produce a huge cheroot made of coarse tobacco and stuffed with dirty sugar, bits of wood and tobacco stalks, and proceed to light and smoke away as if for dear life. It is very surprising, but these abominations do not appear to have any deleterious effect on the precocious youngsters.

Here is a little group of roadside ivory-workers, mere babies all of them, using tools both rough and few, yet their work is surpassingly beautiful and accurate. One of the older ones is giving his baby brother his first lesson; it consists in learning to pick up the tools with his feet, for after he has actually begun to carve, he would be everlastingly disgraced were he to stop work to pick up anything which had fallen to the ground. See! he has dropped a tool now; his eyes do not appear even to move from his work, and his fingers never cease their labours till the missing object is nimbly reached for, lifted by the outstretched foot, and immediately handed to himself by the child with a gravity and dexterity which leaves you speechless. Such are the "four-handed" children of Berhampoor. As we pass along we catch many glimpses of Hindu every-day life. Every little settlement has its own peculiar customs. The oldest dwellers in the land are the Non-Aryans, whom their fair-skinned, stately Aryan vanquishers called "slaves," "flat-nosed," "raw eaters." They are the descendants of the stone and bone men, and you will see any number of them on your walk to the schoolhouse. Yonder are some of the stone circles, slabs and mounds under which their ancient dead are buried, and here are the people themselves.

This bevy belongs to the tribe of the Máris—the most timid tribe in all India. When the Raja's messenger comes once a year to collect their tribute, he never dreams of entering their grass-built huts, but beats a drum and hides himself at some little distance. The Máris creep out and place their jungle products in the appointed spot, then fly back again to their retreats. Their neighbours the Gonds are much more

Hindu cromlech and dolmen.

civilized and are amongst the cleverest hunters in the great "Centre-land." To the right live the "Leaf-wearers" of Orissa, a very poor tribe. Until a few years ago the only garment worn by the women was a bunch of leaves; then a great reformation took place. An officer from the country of the Great White Queen called the whole tribe together, made a speech, and presented each woman with a strip of calico. After a short interval they formed in procession—single file—and made obeisance to him in their new costumes. Then they solemnly collected their old clothes into one great heap and made a bonfire of them. The Santals

are near neighbours of the "Leaf-wearers," but come
of a much higher stock. They have no caste, and as
regards marriage, they consider it best left alone till
the young people are old enough to choose for them-

Indian fiddle and knife.

selves. The Kondhs, on the other hand, a sturdy,
patriarchal hill-tribe, still adhere to the ancient customs
of blood-revenge, child-marriage and the like. When
a Kondh father thinks his son ought to be married, he
looks about for a nice girl some years older than the

boy and strong enough to do her work as a servant in
the old home.   Then a feast is given, during which the
bridegroom forcibly carries off the bride.   The father-
in-law, however, gives a fair price for her, and the
bargain is amicably settled.   As the bride is married
at fourteen and the groom at ten, the former lives
under the dominion of her mother-in-law, till her
husband is old enough to make a separate home for
her.

Native silver jewellery.

But here we are at the school-house.   The master is
a Brahmin and quite charmed to see us.   This is of
course a better class school, and has descended from
father to son for many generations.   Over the way are
some of a poorer character, held under the pipal trees,
but the children are all taught in much the same way.
The seniors are busy with their pen or colours, and
the very little boys who have not yet got the length of
palm-leaf copy-books, draw figures and letters with
their fingers on the sandy floor. Girls don't go to
school at all, for the Hindu does not believe in the

higher education of women, so whatever they learn is
learnt at home. Pop your head into the women's
quarter and you will see something of Hindu young
ladies' education. Two are busy at embroidery frames,
one using filoselle, the other gold for the embellishment
of those beautiful scarves which will make some fair
western belle happy, I take it. Another sister is en-

Hindu silver filigree-work.

gaged with her cookery book, and our olfactory nerves
already foretell a satisfactory result. Before the open
house door a loom is swung between two acacia-trees,
and the yellow blossoms fall like a shower of gold upon
the maiden's hair as she deftly weaves her red and blue
and green threads. Under the verandah sits the
mother with her youngest born upon her knee, and she
tells to her busy daughters the beautiful old legends

they know and love so well.   The story of the fatal

Gold embroidery on velvet.

ring given to the lovely Brahmin maiden Sakuntala,
by the great Rajah Dushyanta, who wooed and wedded

U

her in the forest. How Sakuntala lost the ring—
because a Brahmin had cursed it—and her husband
could no longer recognize her. How for years she
wandered in the jungle with her little son Bharata,

Shams-i-Tabrez of Multan.

till one day the Rajah came to hunt there and saw
Bharata playing with some lions, and knew he must be
his own son. How he sought out Sakuntala, who had
at last found the precious jewel, and how they lived

and reigned happy ever after, and Bharata their son became the conqueror of all India. Then she tells them of the great battle of the Kauravas and Pándavas.

The flying throne of star-taught Kuhimun.

descendants of Bharata; the tales of Rama and Sita, and many more time-honoured legends of gods and men. They all laugh as she describes how Shams-i-Tabrez, a great saint from Baghdad who used to beg

U 2

his bread from door to door, came one day to Multán,
and there caught a fish. He was a very hungry saint,
for bread had been scarce, yet he could not manage to

Prince Siddhártha. Colossal figure from the Yusafzai Valley,
now in Lahore Museum.

eat raw fish, so he prayed the sun to come and cook it.
That obliging luminary came near enough to do so, and
Multán has never been cool since! There is also the

legend of the flying throne of Solomon. That monarch was once travelling in India and fell in love with a beautiful maiden who consented to marry him. They started for their honeymoon on a gorgeous throne carried through the air by genii, and just as they arrived over the summit of a high mountain the lady demanded to be set down that she might take a last look at her old home. Her good-natured husband at once acceded to her request, and the mountain is to this day a favourite shrine of the faithful. Saints are nearly as plentiful as gods in India, but their exploits are not always as saintly as they might be. Everybody knows how on one occasion the behaviour of a certain holy man did not satisfy the governor of his district. The saint was consigned to the nearest oven, and was shortly afterwards found there composedly eating up the roast meat.

Last of all the house-mother relates the sacred story of the good Buddha. Siddhârtha or Gautama was the only son of his father, King Suddhodana, and of his mother, Queen Maya. The king was a great warrior, but Gautama was a thoughtful boy and shunned the world. Nevertheless he was skilful with the bow, and won the glorious Yasodhara for his wife at a famous tournament. Still, he envied the hermit his quiet life, and after ten years, when Yasodhara had borne him a son, he stole softly past his wife's chamber in the night, fearful that the caress of his babe might tempt him back, and departed into the darkness. His royal raiment he changed for the yellow habit of the hermit-beggar, and for six years he wasted himself in the jungle of Gaza. Then he said, " The highest life is not that of self-torture, but to preach the truth to all men," and Gautama became Buddha "the Enlightened," and rose up and preached throughout the land his most excellent law. Now the new-born son whom Buddha had left was converted to his father's faith,

and Yasodhara the beautiful was the first Buddhist
nun.   And after forty and four years Buddha bid fare-

The Great Renunciation.   In the upper part the prince rests with
Yasodhara on a couch; female minstrels attending.   In the
lower division the princess sleeps while Gautama steals away.
(Buddhist fragment from Yusufzai Valley.)

well to the people and foretold his death, saying, "Be
earnest, be thoughtful, be holy.   Keep steadfast watch

over your own hearts, for he who holds fast the law
and discipline, and faints not, he shall cross the ocean
of life and make an end of sorrow. No more shall I
speak to you, I desire to depart. I desire the eternal
rest." And Buddha died there, under the shadow of a
fig-tree, and his last words were, "Work out your
salvation with all diligence."

As I told you before, you cannot understand a Hindu

Buddhist relic casket.

till you know his gods, and I wish I had time to introduce more of them to you—Brahma, Vishnu, Siva; and
to tell you of the four great castes which issued from
the first of these. From his mouth came the Brahmins, having wisdom to pray, read, and teach; from
his arms the Ketterees, having strength to fight and
govern; from his thighs, the Bhyse, to till the ground;
and from his feet the Soudra, to labour and serve.
The four great castes are subdivided into eighty-four,

Buddhist idols and symbols.

Some Hindu gods.

but the Brahmin alone knows the language of the Vedas and understands the mysteries of the sacred religion.

Copper-gilt sacrificial vase.

But the afternoon is creeping on.   The girls fold up their looms, and, with their pitchers on their heads, go to draw water from the tank.

It is quite still in the street now; the children have

gone home; the silversmiths are silent; only the low-
ing of the kine is heard as they are driven across the
plain. But as we pass away from the Island of the

Tea-pot of rich design.

Rose Apple, there rise behind us the voices of the
good priests who sit in the gate and sing the evening
songs from the Rig- and Sama-Vedas of the great
" Centre-land."

CHAPTER IX.

THE CHILDREN OF FUJI SAN.

" What a beautiful country Japan must be,"
Said my little daughter, thoughtfully,
As she studied the views on her fan.
" It has red and white skies, and a mountain blue,
It has green and white grass, and pink trees too;
Did you know trees were pink in Japan?"

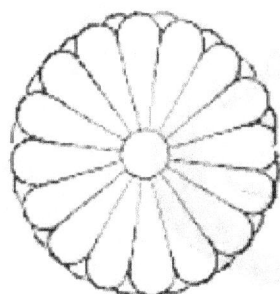

Kiku-mon,
Imperial badge of Japan.

ONCE upon a time the great god Izanagi sat with his wife, the goddess Izanami, watching the waves that rolled beneath their great white cloud-throne. And after a time they said to one another, " Behold, let us bring land from out this sea; let us create a place whereon we can descend and see what things exist in the world that is far off."

And Izanagi dipped his spear into the waters, and lo, the drops that fell as he gathered it to himself again, hardened, and became solid land—each drop an island, in number nearly two thousand. But between the land that Izanagi had made and his throne of cloud, there was a vast space, and as he considered how he might pass from heaven to earth, Izanami wept, crying, " Alas that Izanagi's labour is turned to naught; where-

fore is his wife a looker-on and no helpmeet—a goddess,
and without the imagination to say 'here is a way'?"
And two great tears fell from Izanami's eyes. Down
they rolled, taking into their limpid depths something
of the azure from heaven's own vault; and as they
dropped, the king of the lower air clothed them in a
great garment of mist, white and beautiful, through
which the blue and pearl shone with a radiance born
of Izanami herself. And as they approached the earth
the sea rose and cast about them a veil of pure emerald,
whose hem reached even unto the fringe of the mist-
king's robe. And Izanami's tears became a peerless

Japanese crane, an emblem of longevity.

mountain, majestic, incomprehensible, which rose and
touched the sacred feet of the gods, so that it bridged
the space betwixt heaven and earth. As Izanami
descended, she spread her divine mantle upon the
summit, and there you may see it, spotless unto this
day.

Now on this earth which they had made, Izanagi and
Izanami created living beings of all kinds to inhabit the
place. To themselves were born many children, chiefest
of whom was Amaterasu, the great sun-goddess, who
became the divine mother of all the Mikado. But darkness prevailed on the earth, and Izanami said, "Let

now our first-born, Amaterasu, arise and go to her place in the heavens, that the brightness of her face may be seen over the whole world." And Izanagi consented. So Amaterasu soared high above the peerless mountain, lighting up the snowy mantle with a glory unspeakable, and chasing the darkness away for ever from the habitations of men. After this was the land of Izanagi and Izanami called "Nippon," the Rising Sun, and there, under the shadow of the matchless mountain, the beneficent mother, dwell her ever loving and adoring children.

Such is the Japanese Genesis.

These Easterns are blest with an imagination equal to any emergency, and looking round at the manifold charms of the "Islands of the Dragon-fly," you must admit that they really have something to build on, and may well be forgiven the high-flown names with

Kiri-mon,
the badge of the Mikado's family.

which they have saddled their country. For my part I have always—quite sub rosa, you understand—called it Topsey-Turveydom, and if you don't fall in with my private views before the day is out, my name is not what it is!

In my young days a good deal of trouble was expended in instilling into me the fact that there is a right and a wrong way of doing everything. Since I came to Japan I have had my early ideas so totally upset, and my mind so unhinged, that I couldn't now for the life of me venture to say which is the right and which the wrong. Cuts without tails may not be new, but how would you like to see horses that stand in their stalls with their heads to the street? What do you think of people who water their gardens from a little bucket with a wooden spoon, and who squeeze their own hands and not yours when you happen to meet? I have even seen a gentleman executing wonderful variations on the flute with his nose. The left hand is the place of honour, the birds seldom sing, and kissing is unknown. In fact, if you are ever at a loss as to how any operation should be carried out, just decide what you would consider the proper method, and then proceed to do exactly the opposite. At your elbow there is the carpenter's shop: of course the worthy man planes his wood *towards* instead of *from* him. Two doors off sits the joiner making a utensil of some kind; as you might expect, *he* also saws *to* instead of *from* him.

"Give them a hint," did you say? Not if I know it! It may be very exasperating to watch such outlandish practices, but when you suggest interference, all I can say is "don't." It will be somewhat embarrassing when you discover that their "wrong" way produces quite as satisfactory results as your "right"! Indeed, I may possibly take the liberty of asking you to note some special points where both you and I might, with great advantage, adopt the Japanese custom; so take my advice and leave well alone. Instead of finding fault with what does not concern you, come into the market place, and please to keep your eyes and ears open when you are there.

Here in Yeso, which is a rather neglected part of Dai Nippon, the people are strong and broad—and very hairy! They are the oldest dwellers in all the land, and actually you find them still living in all the primitive simplicity of those early days. They have taken up many strange gods since then, it is true; the bear, the water, the fire, and the four

A flute-player.

winds, but otherwise they have changed very little
during all these centuries. They are hunters and
fishers, soft of speech and gentle in manners; men of
peace who, when another people, smooth, and of small
stature, came and dwelt among them, made no com-
plaint, but crept further and further back, and suffered
the new comers to take whatever they would, till these
last possessed themselves of the whole land save the
morsel of ground on which the hairy men had taken
refuge.

Now I want you to spend a few minutes among the
Ainu before chumming up with their more enlightened
conquerors and successors up the street. The chief of

Ainu dwelling.

the tribe lives in the house over the way there; what
do you say to paying him a surprise visit?

Here we are. Everybody turns out to give us good-
day, bustling about this way and that in their eager-
ness to anticipate our every possible—and impossible
—want. The hut looks like an oblong bee-hive,
being made of reeds neatly bound together over a
frame of wood. The windows are small and the roof is
of thatch, laid on in flounces! Adjoining the hut is
another—its counterpart on stilts; this is the storehouse, an indispensable adjunct to an Ainu habitation.

Now go inside. The family, as you perceive, are at

x

dinner, but that doesn't matter; they will not be in the least put out by seeing you.

We enter by a sort of ante-room in which are kept the millet mill and sundry other culinary appliances. Passing through this, we come to the principal room, nearly thirty feet long, with the fire in the middle. Over the fire swings the pot for the family dinner. It smells vilely; not a surprising fact seeing that "intilt" are sea-weed, beans, wild roots, venison, millet, slugs, bears' flesh, stale, very stale fish, and all lubricated with some equally stale fish oil. There is no table;

Ainu at home.

the diners sit round the fire cross-legged, and this mess of abominations is ladled out into lacquer bowls and handed round. Clay soup, too, is a delicacy much esteemed. It is made of a putty-like clay from the valley, boiled with lily-roots and strained before using.

After the stew comes the "saké," a sort of rice beer, also served out in lacquer bowls, and across the top of which are laid "saké" sticks. These are dipped into the "saké" before drinking, and waved several times towards the fire and the other household gods; this is an Ainu libation. You didn't notice the gods before? You mean you didn't recognize them; a wooden post

dressed in curly, white shavings is not exactly an awe-
inspiring object, but there are several in every Ainu
dwelling, and very much made of they are!

The Ainus, as I said before, are hairy men, so hairy
as to look perfectly ferocious, but the instant they
turn their gazelle-like eyes on you, you begin to like
them; and when they speak, the low music of an
Ainu voice and the sweetness
of an Ainu smile are irresistible; your surrender is complete; you are astonished,
charmed, and altogether
captivated. They are a fascinating and remarkable
people, utter savages in
appearance and in all the
habits of daily life, yet
exhibiting a gentleness and
true politeness to one another which many a cul-
tured nation might copy
with profit. They meet you
always with graceful saluta-
tions; their finest mats
and skins are arranged for
your comfort, and you can
not insult them more deeply
than by offering to pay for
their courteous and eager
hospitality—unless perhaps by looking in at their
windows. In Ainuland this is an unpardonable rude-
ness. Please make a note of this! Should you propose to buy any of their simple handiwork, they either
only accept half of what you offer or decline remunera-
tion altogether.

Ainu women are not quite as good-looking as their
male relations, and the manner in which they tattoo

Ainu gods.

X 2

themselves does not improve things by any means.
But they are never idle, and their position in the
family is much higher than that held by women in
most primitive communities. They are even allowed
to sell whatever bark-cloth they can make beyond that
needed to clothe the household, and their husbands
never dream of taking their earnings from them. This
bark weaving is their chief occupation, the men bringing them the bark from the woods in five-feet strips,
with the outer coating all ready removed. The various
layers of the inner bark are then separated, the fibres
split, very neatly knotted and wound into balls. It is
woven into webs fifteen feet long by fifteen inches wide,
and all the knots are carefully kept on the under-side.
The loom is the simplest in existence. To a hook in
the floor is fixed one end of the web; the threads are
tightened by being fastened to the weaver's waist, and
are kept separate by a rude comb laid across the ankles,
while a wooden roll divides the upper and under threads
and allows the worker to pass her wooden shuttle back-
wards and forwards with great rapidity.

But we have stayed longer in Yeso than I bargained
for, and must leave the gentle bear-worshippers behind.
The palings all round the hamlet are crowned with
bear skulls, and the only real rival this grizzly denizen
of the woods has in Ainu esteem is the peeled wand
with the fringe of shavings!

Surely this is not a band of drunken men we meet
at the end of the village? Ah! I wish I had got you
safely off before the cloven hoof peeped out. Yes,
these mild, amiable savages have one curse, and it is—
"saké." No shop so popular as the saké-shop; no
sacrifice so acceptable to the gods as saké-drinking.
Alas, what hope is there for men whose whole religion
is embodied in "drinking to the gods"? Their past is
dead, for they do not even know their own ages, and so
long as intoxication continues to form their only expres-

A " sui:ô " shop

sion of worship, so long will the Ainu be a mournful
example of a futureless people—a decaying race, passing
slowly, but surely, into an everlasting limbo.

From the huts of Yeso to the streets of Yedo—Tôkio
they call it now—is rather a far call. The roads round
Tôkio too are certainly both rough and dirty, but
when you reach the streets you are no less astonished
than delighted, they are so spick and span. Not an
inch of dust nor even a stray scrap of paper in these
immaculate streets! Would you like to know how
they manage it? Let me introduce the Kamikud-
subiroi. He doesn't rank very high in the social scale,
I admit, but when you are seeking for information you
haven't to be too particular. The "picker-up-of-
scraps" is rather a grotesque-looking person, from the
fact that he is clad in a garment entirely made of
patches. Rag leggings, tied on with very many pieces
of rope, and a huge reed hat complete his usual attire,
excepting that his face is covered to the eyes with a
blue cotton handkerchief. He is a sort of human
jackal, prowling round dust-heaps and dark corners
with his sticks and his basket; but you are much
beholden to him for clean and tidy streets. He belongs
to the class called *Éta*, upon whom falls all the dirty
work of the town: the burying of dead dogs, cleaning
out of cesspools, attendance on criminals, and so forth.

His shreds of dirty paper go first to the waste-paper
shops, and, when thoroughly sorted, to the Kamiskiya
or paper-mill. I doubt whether I can show you the
paper-mill to-day, but the process of paper-making is
very primitive in Japan. The old paper is reduced to
pulp about the colour of very dirty water, and of the
consistency of cream, and run into troughs. A woman
stands before each trough with a bamboo sieve, which
she dips into the fluid until a fairly even layer of pulp
is deposited in it. She then sets it on edge to drain.
When a good many sieves have been used she returns

A sketch from the outskirts of Pekin.

to the first, removes the sheet of paper to a board and
lays it out to dry in the sun. Every layer is treated
in this way, and when quite hardened, the whole are
packed up in bundles and are ready for the dealer.
This is, of course, only common paper—there are
really about sixty different kinds made in Japan, each
having its own clearly defined use. One variety
is for pictures, another for windows, a third for
cloaks, and a fourth for tea-cups; fancy a paper tea-
cup!

I am not sure that you will think the later children
of Fuji San quite as sweet-spoken as their Ainu
brothers, but they are both pleasant and gentle-*looking*,
and believe me, they do not belie their looks. I don't
think you will ever find a more delightful companion
than the gentlemanly Japanese. Being a stranger in
those parts, you find it difficult to tell the women from
the men, so to save a scandal, I had better point out
some of the distinguishing features.

The dress is nearly alike for both sexes, and consists
of a rather "scimp" dressing-gown called a "Kimono,"
which makes up in sleeves what it lacks in skirt.
These sleeves are partly sown up to form capacious
pockets, into which a whole wardrobe might very easily
be stowed away. The Kimono is fastened from left
to right by both ladies and gentlemen. Round the
waist goes the "Obi," a girdle worn narrow by males
and wide and long by females, and requiring quite an
education to adjust. The arrangement proper for a
young lady won't do at all when she gets married.
Age and social position have also to be considered in
adjusting the Obi, which, by the way, forms another
excellent and roomy pocket. No underlinen is worn,
but beneath the Kimono are a sort of vest and jacket,
both of them as shapeless as you could well conceive.
The socks, like the gloves of our infancy, have a division
for the biggest digit, and this allows for the tightening

The Kaeikadeubiroi.

up of the cords which fasten on those wooden clogs that sometimes give the Japanese such a fictitious height. In wet weather cloaks of straw for peasants and labourers, of oiled paper for artisans and tradesmen, and of very thick dark blue cotton for all persons of the better class, are brought to light, and I must not forget the inevitable fan, used by both sexes and on all occasions. The fan serves every purpose under the sun: beggars hold it out for charity, the dude uses it as a switch, and the schoolmaster as a rod for the schoolboys' knuckles.

You have then the width and length of the Obi to distinguish the sexes by, but you are still in doubt? Look at their hair. The women's is done up in the most elaborate bobs and loops; the men, on the contrary, shave their hair back so far that their foreheads may safely be said to reach almost to the nape of their necks, and the few locks that are left are combed up into a tight knot on the crown. I should say this was the fashion, for the majority of Japanese gentlemen now wear their hair exactly as you do. Shaving where you come from is one thing, and in Japan quite another. We will drop in at the barber's as we pass, and you can see the old-fashioned process for yourself. The worthy man stands flourishing his razor ready for action: on a bench before him sits his patron, a gentleman who abjures all new-fangled notions. After a preliminary combing which, every hair being in perfect order, seems quite unnecessary, the shaving begins. Such expert shaving you never saw before! It is marvellous to witness the calmness of the subject and the deftness of the operator. What an artist that barber is! You would imagine the case called out every resource of mind and body. It is all affectation though, that bustle of his, and meant to delude you into the belief that a crowd of waiting customers necessitates the utmost despatch on his part. He

The barber.

passes the time of day and many a sly joke too with every passer-by, and you actually tremble to see his eyes fixed on some chattering idiot in the street while the knife is dodging from ear to nostril, and from nostril to eyebrow of the complacent customer. Don't alarm yourself, not a drop of blood will be shed. He is thoroughly wide awake, and finishes his work with a dramatic bow and a complimentary remark on the improved visage of his patron, dismisses him with a flourish of trumpets and—"Next for shaving!"

Do be careful, my good fellow! You have sent me spinning against a poor boy flying a kite here at the barber's door. The child makes me a profound bow and goes on with his kite-flying; truly politeness reigns supreme in Japan! Just watch how the youngster tries to get his kite into such a position that its string will gradually saw through that of his neighbour. Ah, he has done it! Three very low bows are exchanged between the rival boys, and the out kite becomes the victor's prize. Quite a score of tiny tots have come out to see the fun, and I assure you they are thoroughly enjoying it, in spite of their solemn little faces; but it does seem a shame to let such mites run out alone. Well, I never! Each of them has a beautifully designed card attached to his waist, with name and address fully inscribed thereon. What a boon to policemen! You might be kind enough to take this down as note number two.

It is the fashion here to carry on the sale of special goods in special streets. We are now passing along the hair-pin street; next to it is the fan street, and the turning beyond leads you to the toy street, while that space round the corner might be called the prayer street, for it boasts at least two temples, and some say a prayer-wheel once stood at the corner itself.

There are two religions in Japan—"Shinto" or ancestor worship, and Buddhism, the religion of

Buddha, which has travelled to the children of Fuji San from the Island of the Rose Apple. "Shinto" is much the older of the two, and on it are based nearly all the laws and customs governing Japanese society. It enjoins reverence for the sun-goddess, and outside that Shinto temple you will see a straw rope fastened round one of the pillars. This is the explanation thereof. Once the sun-goddess Amaterasu was deeply offended by some act of a scamp of a brother she had, and hid herself in a cavern. This turned day into night and caused a vast deal of confusion; so the other gods agreed together to entice her out. It is said that they first invented music for this laudable end; at any rate, out she came, and they thereupon closed the cave with a straw rope, which has ever since been sacred to her, and is found outside every Shinto temple.

But according to Hirata Atsutane—the Martin Luther of Shinto—devotion to the memory of ancestors is the mainspring of all virtues, and the very essence of it is filial piety. Now, such devotion to ancestors involves reverence for, and fulfilment of, every duty to their descendants, the living members of the household, hence love and reverence are the two props on which the whole family system of Japan is built. The father is the *Ko Shu*, "House Master," and he is an absolute ruler. He performs the part of family magistrate, and is an object of wholesome fear as well as respect to those urchins, his children. The mother governs more by love than fear, and in consequence of this somewhat bitter-sweet upbringing you will often hear the little rascals talking of the "strict father," and the "benevolent mother"; while the four fearful things in the world are classified by juvenile Japan as "earthquake," "thunder," "conflagration," and— "father"! But in spite of all this, Dai Nippon *is* still "the Children's Paradise," the land where the babies never cry. They are loaded with toys and

sweets, and once a year boys and girls have each a
special festival at which the elders devote themselves
entirely to the enjoyment of the little ones. These all
go to school, to be sure, and you may see them any
day you like, as busy as possible with their lesson-
books, beginning at the end and reading down the
page instead of across it, but there is neither force used
nor haste demanded in the school, and without either a
"cole" or a "persuader," every child in Japan becomes
master of the three R's. The school "fixings" are not
at all what you are accustomed to. Yonder are displayed the signs of the Zodiac; not "the ram, the bull,
the heavenly twins," but the rat, ox, tiger, and rabbit;
dragon, serpent, horse, and goat; monkey, cock, dog,
and hog; and what takes you still more by surprise is to
see master and children alike provided with minute
pipes and smoking like furnaces! The examinations,
as might be expected, come after, not before the holidays, in topsey turveydom, and the personal names, I
might add, follow the same rule and come after the
surname. The little girls often bear the names of
favourite objects in nature, "Cherry Blossom," "Snow,"
"Summer"; truth compels me to add that as it is the
custom to name them after the first object the mother
casts her eyes on after the little one is born, they run
equal risk of having a very inappropriate, not to say
ugly appellation tacked on to them. "Frying pan"
and "Dust brush" are the names of two such pretty
little maidens over the way!

But we are forgetting the temples we walked over
here to see. This one is sacred to Kwannon, the
Buddhist goddess of mercy. She is a great favourite,
and there are always streams of people coming in to
say their prayers.

A man beside you going on in a disgraceful way, did
you say? Positively pelting the goddess with chewed-
up balls of paper! Well, you don't appear to know

A mecsside surlus

much of the ways round here; did you never hear that on the papers he munches the devout Japanese writes his prayers, and that this is the approved method of offering them to his divinity? If they stick to her, the prayers are answered, if not—well, he must spit out a few more till they do.

Japan abounds more in gods than goddesses, which may account, to some extent, for the respect accorded to Kwannon and Benten, and I must on no account neglect to mention those ever-present divinities, The Gods of Good Fortune. There are seven of them :—

1. Fukurokujiu, god of longevity, distinguished by a big head, long beard, a tortoise and a stork.

2. Hotei, god of contentment, a dear old fat god, whose delight is in playing with children.

3. Daikoku, god of riches, whose miner's hammer and bales of rice suggest the sources of Japan's wealth.

4. Yebis, god of daily bread, especially fish; this being a favourite food in Japan.

5. Bishamon, god of prosperity and military glory, usually dressed as an armed warrior.

6. Juro-jin, a very learned-looking figure, sometimes looked on as another form of Fukurokujiu.

7. Benten, goddess of love, generally wearing a diadem and rich trailing robes.

You will find one or other of them in every house, and forming the subject of endless legends, adventures, and art works of every kind.

Then there are those mischievous little imps, the *Oni*, or demons, whose antics alternately amuse and aggravate the unoffending people they haunt. Every now and then, particularly on New Year's Day, the *Oni* receive special attention and are pelted off the premises with beans.

There are forest, as well as domestic demons in Japan, but they are a very harmless race of beings, and nobody meddles with them.

Not far from you sits a Jeso or "Succourer." It has a lapful of pebbles to play with, and a bib tucked under its chin. This is the kind-hearted god that helps babies through their teething troubles.

The Buddhists have invented many labour-saving dodges in the way of praying machines. In the temple adjoining that of Kwannon, there is a revolving room containing all the sacred writings of the great Gautama. It takes a pretty stiff push to send it round, but it is worth the effort, for one turn is equal to reading the whole library through!

Among other peculiarities is one which strikes you very forcibly in Dai Nippon, namely, the evident predilection for numbers. You have already heard of the "*four* fearful things of the world," but there is a host of other combinations equally fascinating: the *five* festivals; the *seven* jewels; the *eight* beautiful sights; and the *six and thirty* poets; while the proverb which says that he who dreams of Fuji, *two* falcons and *three* egg-plants, will have a long and prosperous life, exhibits the same fancy.

But all this is, after all, only in keeping with people who are poetical and artistic to their very finger-tips. I could tell you a thousand beautiful legends which show even the commonplace occurrences of every-day life glorified with the halo of poetry and romance which crowns this delightful land. Pray do not fail to read the "Story of the Tongue-cut Sparrow" if ever you see it!

We want now to see the children of Fuji San at home, and I have my eye on a house that I think I can smuggle you into. The noises are really deafening in the street:—"Amma, Kami Shitmo, ni-ju-shi mon," yells the bathing man, which being interpreted, means that he will knead you from top to toe for twenty-four "mon" or half a farthing, and if you are at all inclined to be rheumatic, you might do worse

Y

than engage one of those blind shampooing and bathing men. The house we are going to is a light frame-
work building with a heavy roof. It has only two
stories—very few Japanese houses have more—but the
rooms are a good size. The one we enter first is a
room of "eight mats," and one of the first things you
learn about Japanese dwellings is that the mats, or
rather mattresses, which cover every floor, are of so
uniform a size that they are used as a standard

A fragile dwelling.

measure. They are six feet three inches long by
three feet two inches wide, very much the size of
your own hearthrug, and vary from two and a half
to four inches thick, and as they are never cut, the
rooms are always made to fit the mats, and never
the mats to fit the floor. Rooms of four, six, or twelve
mats become quite intelligible when you know this.
The partitions are all removable, and generally of
sliding laths, covered over in some cases with thin
matting. Every dwelling has its altar or domestic

shrine, before which the household renders daily devotion to its ancestors. The best rooms are at the back of the house, but there is next to no furniture in any of them, the principal items being the " Hibachi " or portable brazier, and the " Tabako-bon," a tray with a vessel of glowing fuel and a spittoon. A few " Kakemono " or scroll pictures are hung round, and there are numberless cupboards and lacquered boxes to hold the bedding, which is never brought out till bed-time. In the sleeping-rooms you will see no beds, and the bedding consists of a mattress stuffed with wadding, a pillow, and a nightgown. The pillow is a curiosity : a stool without feet, having a semicircular piece cut out for the neck, and over this a small padded roll and a paper pillow-slip !

Houses being of wood, fires are always a plentiful crop, but nobody minds them much, and certainly nobody expects to begin and end his days in the same house. There are no insurance agencies, so when a man is burnt out, he simply looks to his nearest relations to set him going again. They never dream of objecting, knowing full well that their turn may come within the week.

We really ought to be going now, but our host will be greatly insulted if we do not stay to share the meal that is about to be served. It is an extra special feast to-day, for the younger daughter of the house is just betrothed to a very desirable parti, and with that loving desire to give pleasure which is so typical of Japan, the various families are celebrating the double event here in grand style. At one time the lover had the privilege of proposing direct to the lady of his choice, but now it is considered comme il faut to engage Go-betweens, who are selected from both families to arrange various preliminaries. These meet together, and with great solemnity choose two auspicious days, the first for the interview between the lady

and her suitor, and the second for the wedding.
Where no Go-between is employed, the love-lorn youth
does his own courting. He declares his passion by
hanging a branch of a certain shrub against the door
of his fair one's house, and sits down to await the
dénouement. If the branch be neglected, the match is
not to the lady's mind; but if accepted, so is the lover.
With our young folks here all preliminaries have been
settled for them, and they have only now to do as they
are told. This pleases them very well, so you may
spare them your commiserations at having so little
choice in this most vital step. The expectant bridegroom has sent his presents of dried cuttle-fish, sea-
weed, flax, and "saké" not to mention a fine new
"Obi," to the bride, who promptly handed them over
to her parents.

The hammer of Daïkoku, God of Riches.

But while we are chattering, the dinner is waiting.
It is spread on the floor, and each guest has a cushion to
himself, and sits around on his heels. Before each is a
table only six inches high, arranged with various lacquer
trays and bowls from which to eat. As you go forward to
take your cushion, you are quite puzzled to understand
the meaning of that retinue of servants standing about
with immense baskets. Our host informs us that those
are not of his household at all, but have been brought
by the guests to carry away the remnants of the feast.
It is very vulgar to leave anything on the table after

a banquet, and what you can't eat you are bound to carry away if you wish to be considered well-bred.

There is a good deal of formality about the beginning of a Japanese feast, but as the " saké " circulates, tongues begin to wag and compliments to fly, and soon there is a general hilarity which infects even you. This is a suitable occasion for the display of valuable pieces of lacquer and china, and no compliment is so flattering as outspoken admiration of the table ware and inquiries as to the prices of the various objects. Quite like a banquet in Lotus-land !

Now do give some attention to your dinner; the servants have piled a portion of every dish into your bowl, and are waiting to pass you—when you are ready—condiments and sauces of various kinds, while close to your hand stands your well-filled rice-bowl and your chopsticks. Let me read you the menu :—

1. Shellfish soup, with pears.
2. Stewed mushrooms and chrysanthemum blossoms.
3. Fried eels and relishes.
4. Grilled cod and ditto.
5. Fried fish of another sort.
6. Fowls.
7. Savoury omelette.
8. Raw fish.
9. Stewed mixed vegetables and seaweed.
10. Stewed shell-fish and pickles.
11. Rice.
12. Hot "saké."

Fish, you will have gathered, is the standing dish ; it is the roast beef of Japan, and has come to be so in memory of the ancestors, whose chief diet it formed. Eggs sometimes find their way to table also, but milk, cheese, and butter are abominations to the children of the peerless mountain. Many of the dishes are decked out with gold leaf, and the beak, legs, and claws of the poultry are also gilded. The " saké " is drunk out of

little cups without handles, and is taken warm. As
the dinner draws to a close the newly-engaged damsel
entertains the company with a song, accompanying
herself on the samisen, or three-stringed guitar, and
one or two of the seniors slip off to a quiet game at
chess or draughts, cards and dice being prohibited in
respectable Japan!

I have no doubt that, having been interested in the
betrothal of a Japanese maiden, you would now like
to see one married. I am sorry I can't oblige you,
because weddings take place at night in Japan, and
we shall bid adieu to the beautiful dragon-fly before
that time.

But do not look so disconsolate, I will tell you all
about it, and you can follow me in imagination to the
grand *finale*.

Although no dowry is given her, the bride does not
go empty-handed to her husband ; after a solemn
burning of all her dolls, her parents send, some days
ahead, a liberal trousseau, a loom, spinning-wheel,
and much kitchen ware, to await her in her new
home.

Great preparations are made on both sides for a long
time beforehand ; presents of cuttle-fish, sea-weed, flax
and "saké" are exchanged between bride and groom ;
clothes are cut out and made, and all needed articles
purchased for the former, while the latter, on his side,
tidies up his house outside and in, and makes ready a
feast on a grand scale.

At last the auspicious evening comes. We will
accompany the party in the wedding procession, if you
please, but before we start I ought to tell you that
though the family priest may bestow his blessing on
the happy pair, marriage here is merely a civil contract,
and there is no religious ceremony whatever.

The bride is pretty, though she *has* blackened her
teeth, dispensed with the eyebrows she was born with,

and taken to painted ones instead.   At the moment she
leaves the parental home for that of a husband she is
covered from head to foot by her friends with a white
veil, which will afterwards become her shroud.   Seated
in a palanquin, she is carried forth, surrounded by
relations, friends, and Go-betweens, and the pro-

Fukurokujin, god of longevity.

cession makes the tour of the town.   When we
reach the bridegroom's house, we find that gentleman
already there, seated in state with his relations, and
anxiously awaiting our arrival.   In the middle of the
reception-room stands a beautiful table, carved with
fir and pine trees, cranes and tortoises, emblems of

man's strength and women's beauty, as well as of
longevity; while on another table is laid out the
banquet—not forgetting the "saké"!   Beside this the
bride places herself, and then begins such a bowing,
pouring out, presenting and drinking of "saké" as
beggars description.   Stories are told, pranks played,
etc.   Generous libations of "saké" are offered to the
gods, especially to those of good fortune and riches,
and to Fukurokujin, the god of longevity.   The hum
of the story-teller's voice reaches you from the other
room: listen, he is just beginning anew!

"You don't know why the moth flies at the candle?
Then I must tell you about the Princess Hotaru and
her lovers.   Princess Hotaru was a fire-fly and lived in
a lotus.   Every day she grew lovelier and lovelier, and
wherever she went a crowd of suitors followed her.   But
she cared for none of them, and one day she said to her
mother. 'To-night I shall lay an impossible duty on
these adventurers.   If they are wise they will not try
to perform it, yet, if they love their lives more than
me, I want none of them.   At any rate, whoever
succeeds may have me as his bride.'   No sooner had
the twilight faded than forth came a golden beetle, who
made obeisance, and said, 'I am Lord Green and Gold,
and I offer my love and fortune to Princess Hotaru.'
'Go, bring me fire, and I will be your bride,' said
Hotaru.   The beetle opened its wings and departed.
Next came a scarlet dragon-fly: 'Bring me fire,'
repeated the princess; off flew the dragon-fly with a
buzz, and in came a moth to plead his suit.   'I'll say
yes, if you bring me a flash of fire,' said Hotaru.
Suitor after suitor came to woo the princess, and one
after another she sent them away.   Alas! poor suitors!
none ever came back to wed her.   The beetle whizzed
up to a window in which a light gleamed: too full of
love to think of wood or iron, he dashed his head
against a nail and fell dead.   'What's that?' said a

The story-teller.

thrifty housewife at her needle, as her lamp flared up and, being of paper, was instantly burnt. Among the scorched bits she found a roasted dragon-fly! The moth, mad with love, drew nearer and nearer the student's candle flame; now here, now there, he buzzed, then darted forward to snatch a flash of flame, singed his wings and died in agony! 'What a fool he was,' said another moth; 'I'll get the fire.' So he crawled up the candle and got to the top very carefully, when lo! the student snuffed the wick and crushed him to death. Sad indeed was the fate of the lovers! One visited the cremation furnace, another the kitchen; some burned their noses at the top of the incense sticks; others chased the sparks that flew out of the chimney, but none brought fire to the princess or gained the lover's prize. Some only lost feelers, others wings, but the most of them lay stark dead in the morning, and the servant-maids trimming the lamps and candles, each remarked that the Princess Hotaru must have had a great following last night! There were a great many funerals that day, and Himaro, prince of the fire-flies, inquired of the servants the cause. Then he heard for the first time of the lovely Hotaru. He saw her, loved and won her, for she, who was adamant to the vulgar herd, yielded at once to the glitter of the fire-fly prince. So now, my children," concludes the old man, "whenever you see the dead moths round the candle, remember the lovers of the princess Hotaru."

In one corner a renowned fortune-teller keeps a small audience spell-bound as he reveals the destiny of each eager listener; in short, the whole evening is given up to jollification. Three days later the newly-married pair will go to pay their respects to the wife's family, and that ends the wedding formalities.

You do not find it easy to tear yourself away from so much fun, but glad am I to get into the street again,

The fortune-teller.

and we must hurry up if we want to get through our remaining business before sundown. "Call a cab?" My young friend, you may call till you are black in the face; no cab will gladden your eyes here, but you may get into that wooden armchair mounted on wheels if you like, and a wiry little runner will trot you all round the town in an hour. The Japanese "Kuruma" —"Jinrikisha," I should say, for such is the name of this delightful kind of Kuruma or carriage—is a grand insti-

Hen.   Kiyomidzu ware.

tution, but oh, the tattooing of that runner's body! From one foot springs a tree, the branches of which envelop the whole man, and form a happy hunting-ground for scores of birds and insects artfully depicted among the clusters of fruit and flowers. On the other foot a stork complacently stands under the shadow of this remarkable arboricultural production. But he is a sharp-witted fellow, despite his extraordinary appearance, and has a perfectly insane enthusiasm about everything Japanese.

He is brimming over with legends redounding to the
honour and glory of the Land of the Rising Sun. "My
country," says he, stopping at a corner to take breath,
"is the most flourishing and peaceful in all the world.
It is a long time since one of our emperors caused a

Cock. Kiyomidzu ware.

drum to stand outside his palace gates so that the
people might beat and demand redress when they had a
grievance, but everybody was so contented and happy
that the drum was never used, and became the roosting-
place of a cock. A cock and a drum are therefore to
us an emblem always of perfect contentment."

"And our Art," he goes on excitedly, "why, every baby has heard of Kanaoka's horse, painted on a screen in a temple at Kioto. A wonderful horse, so true to nature that in the hours of darkness it would quit its frame and career through all the fields around, till the angry farmers, recognizing it, went in a body to the picture, and finding its guilt confirmed by the mud on its hoofs, ruthlessly blotted out the eyes of the masterpiece. Thenceforward, the nocturnal excursions ceased, and Kanaoka's horse had only a pictorial existence. Over at the Treasury there, was another such creature, a dragon from the same brush, which took to devouring all the flowers within reach, till, happily, the artist tethered it to its panel by a painted rope." And so he goes on, considerably more breathless than when he set you down, and would go on for ever, if you did not hint that

Kanaoka's horse.

you are anxious to reach your destination before midnight.

Allowing for a certain amount of national prejudice, however, he is in the main right; Art holds undisputed sway in Japan, and no wonder! In no part of our street of human habitations are the landscapes more lovely or the flowers more abundant; and so keenly do the people appreciate them, that there are days set apart for nothing else than to admire them. "Beholdings," they call these, and there is one proper to each month. That of the maple, in

Autumn, is known as the "long beholding." or the

Flower vase. Yotsu-shiro ware.

"gazing intently at," but the "cherry beholding,"
in April, is certainly the most delightful. They

know better, too, than to cram as many flowers into
a vase as it will hold; one flower at a time in each

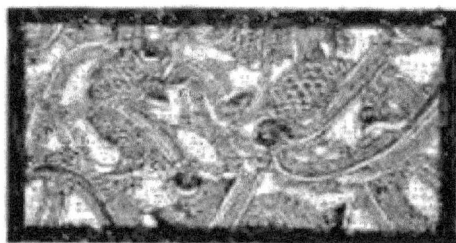

vase is quite enough for *them*, and when this has been
thoroughly enjoyed, another replaces it.

To describe their stencil-work is impossible, for it is

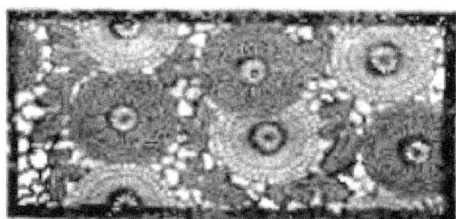

indescribable, and in all but Japanese hands, inimi-
table. At first sight, the lace-like designs look as if they
could not possibly support themselves. but on examina-

tion you find the delicate tracery is held together by hair,
or silken threads as fine as gossamer, and of which the

brush will take no cognizance when the stencil comes to be used. These threads are placed between the two layers of brown paper which compose the stencil, and the layers are then put together in a manner most marvellous, and with an accuracy only to be accomplished, as I said before, by Japanese hands.

Japanese lacquer work, too, is a monument of patience and skill, and when we hear of a background whose drying alone occupied 580 hours; of pure gold inlays and overlays; of skilfully distributed gold and silver dust, each having seven degrees of fineness and covered with a dozen coats of fine lacquer; and of endless polishings after that, we are not so much surprised that the wary Jap thinks twice before allowing the best specimens to leave his country, and considers that even to *show* such to uncultured creatures like you and me is " like giving guineas to a cat."

Until I came here, I was under the impression that in Japan every child was taught to draw natural objects from its earliest years, in school and out of it, and am not a little surprised to find that the artists are, as a rule, confined to certain families, the heads of which each take a number of students to train. These live with their masters during their whole apprenticeship, very often adopt his name, and eventually succeed him. For twelve or thirteen years, from the age of fourteen, they work from 7 a.m. till 10 p.m. every day, not from nature, but in mere mechanical copying of old masters. Each one is given two mats, measuring together about six feet square, in the *atelier*, and on these he has to find room for himself and his working materials; on them he works all day and sleeps at night.

Notwithstanding all their hard work, the children of Fuji San know how to enjoy themselves. They have, at least, one festival every month, and there are five that are especially popular. On the first day of the first month—New Year's Day—they celebrate "the feast of presents," and he is poor indeed, who does not both give and receive on that day. Every man's debts must be paid on the day preceding this feast, so that he begins the year at peace with all his neighbours. On the third of the third month comes the girls' "festival of dolls." Many generations of dolls are brought out, new ones bought, and dolls and children are feasted royally on cakes and "Shiro-saké" by the indulgent parents. The fifth of the fifth month brings the "feast of flags," the boys' own particular carnival. Then drums and trumpets are given them, each with a tiny flag attached, and with which they parade the streets all day. On the seventh of the seventh month, all Japan turns out in honour of the great "feast of lanterns," a most magnificent display, ending up with a brilliant illumination at night. Finally, on the ninth of the ninth month is held the "feast of chrysanthemums," when the blossoms of the national flower are scattered over every cup of tea or "saké" drunk during the day. This celebration conduces to long life—so they say.

A good deal of Japanese time is taken up in writing notes and sending presents, the last being governed by laws as stringent as any in the land. Certain days bring presents as surely as these days come round, and some gifts have a fixed nature and value, while others are left to the donor's choice; but a superior always gives useful, and an inferior merely pretty objects to his friends. Between equals value does not count: a quire of paper or a few eggs are sufficient, if only they be arranged in a nice box, tied with silk cord, and accompanied by a knot of coloured paper to give good luck. Above all, a bit of dried fish must not be forgotten. This goes with every gift, great or small, and is indispensable at the most sumptuous banquets.

Crash! Smash!! What in all the world is the

The doctor.

matter? Dear me, this is very shocking! In turning
a corner we have collided with the biggest dignitary of
the place; the doctor of highest repute in Yedo. You
are shot into the arms of his astonished medicine
carrier, while the kuruma, after nearly cutting the
learned doctor himself in two, is careering down the
street at ten miles an hour. Our botanical friend, the
runner, sits down in the street—broken shaft in hand—
to think the matter over; in about half-an-hour he
will probably recover sufficiently to go after the kuruma,
but I hardly think we can wait for that! Our last
call in Yedo is to a house quite near, so we will dispense
with a conveyance and walk there. We make a series
of profound bows and inquire with great solicitude
after the safety of the doctor and his nostrums. He
goes through the same pantomime, and assures us that
the inconvenience is a mere nothing. "Hurt! Oh,
dear no! Not at all; quite a pleasure, in fact, to make
your acquaintance!" he exclaims. Of course you don't
believe him, and he knows you don't; but still it is a
pleasanter method of meeting a catastrophe than
swearing at it. Off he goes, bowing again and again,
and we continue our journey in an opposite direction.

I said we had one more call to make. So we have;
but it is upon the dead, not the living. To yonder
dwelling the grim visitor has come in his most cruel
garb, he has laid his hand on the most cherished one
there, and at a time the saddest you can think of. A
life for a life; the first faint wail of baby lips, the last
sigh of a dying mother, and in one short hour, a
desolation unspeakable has fallen on the young husband
and father. The little one, so long and so joyously
looked for, is laid in other arms and in a strange
cradle. Her father cannot yet forget how dearly she had
been bought, and they do not remind him of his loss by
keeping the motherless babe about the house. This
is the funeral day, and we are going to join the

Funeral.

mourners. According to custom, all the screens and
sliding doors of the house are turned upside down, all

Incense burner.   Satsuma ware.

garments are worn inside out. The young husband
is too much absorbed in grief to do anything, so

his intimate friends take all arrangements out of his hands, and leave him to weep in unmolested solitude. One lays out the body, another orders the funeral, a third receives the visits of condolence—at the house door, not inside! The grave is dug in the temple grounds. It is like a well, lined with cement, and as the deceased was married, is made large enough for two. Very shortly a monument will be set up, and on it, besides the name of the dead, will be placed that of the survivor in *red*.

The body, in its bridal shroud, is placed, sitting, in a tub-shaped coffin, within which is another of earthenware: then the procession starts. First come the torch-bearers, followed by priests bearing handsome jars of incense; next, the servants with bamboo poles, to which are hung lanterns, umbrellas, and strips of paper inscribed with sacred sentences; then the corpse, in its tub-coffin, on a bier, and covered with a white paper chest, round which flowers are suspended. Directly after the body come all the friends and acquaintances of the male sex, wearing mourning garments of pure white. Male and female kinsfolk follow in palanquins, and the female acquaintances bring up the rear. The procession is met at the temple by a train of priests, and the funeral service is performed, and the corpse buried, to a funeral strain played on a copper basin. During the ceremony two recorders sit in a corner and take down the names of all who have attended. In very early days the house of the dead was always burnt, except so much as was needed to construct a monument to him. Now it is sufficiently purified by kindling an immense fire before it, and burning thereon sweet-scented oils and spices. In these old days, also, the servants were buried alive with a master or mistress: as time and civilization advanced they were allowed to kill themselves before burial, but there was no shirking *that*, and in hiring them it was always

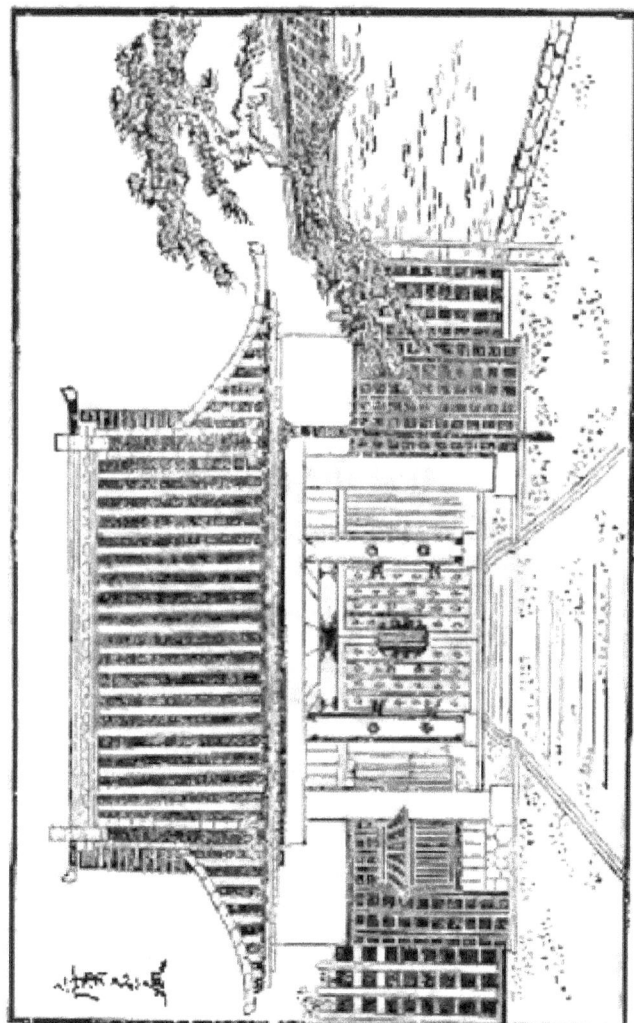

A Gateway.

stipulated that they should thus die should occasion arise? Later on effigies took their place.

We leave the young mother to her last sleep, and turn to join the mourners, who are now going home and expect you to take a solemn cup of tea with them before you bid them adieu.

host goes then to fetch the utensils, assuring us again
and again of his gratification at seeing us.   He carries
in successively a box of charcoal, a pair of tongs, the

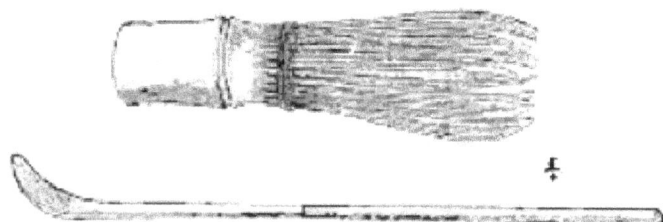

Bamboo whisk and jointed spoon.

kettle-stand, the handles for the same, a box of incense
and some paper.   He next brings a vessel with ashes

Tea jar, Seto ware.

and proceeds to make up the fire, the guests all the
while inspecting and admiring the various objects,
especially those that are antique.   Then the tea-things

come out in the same single file: kettle, tea-stand, tea-jars, fresh water, and a tea-bowl. There is, besides, a bamboo whisk, a jointed spoon, and a purple tea-towel. Very solemnly every article is wiped out, and some tea from a jar is placed in the bowl, hot water poured over, and the whole whisked vigorously. A servant now hands you the bowl and you help yourself. In this way it goes to every guest and returns empty to the host. All the utensils are then washed by that gentle-

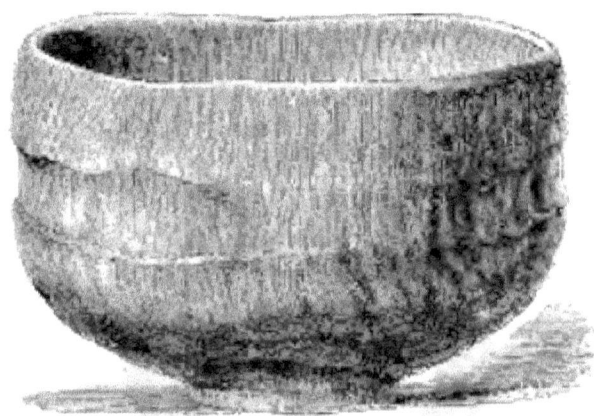

Tea-bowl.

men and passed round for criticism; and the tea-party is at an end.

One last office we have still to perform for the dead. Do you see that piece of linen, suspended by its four corners at the road-side there? It is held up by four stakes driven into the ground; beside it is a bucket of water and a ladle, behind is a panel with a short story on it. Stop! I pray you, and help to release the soul of the unhappy deceased. Here, in Japan, a death, such as this, is believed to come as a judgment for some sin, and so long as

Nagaré Kanjo.

Bewitched.

that linen towel hangs entire so long will the suffering soul be held in bondage. Pour, then, at least one ladleful of pure water into the napkin; every drop passing through helps to wear the linen out, and as soon as the first rupture occurs the troubled spirit will find rest! What passer-by could neglect the "Nagaré Kanjo," or resist the mute appeal to contribute a cup of water for such an object?

I have kept you a long time among the flowers of Dai Nippon; but you do not grudge the time! They tell me I am bewitched by that sly creature, the fox,

Fuji San, the Peerless Mountain.

who is ever on the prowl here, and that I have no heart left for any land less fair. It may be so: the cherry-blossoms, the dragon-flies, the solemn little babies, the soft-voiced Ainu, and above all, Fuji, that mild mother and glorious mountain, have for me a charm beyond words, a fascination unequalled, save by the wondrous Land of the Lotus; and when you have once beheld the dazzling purity of that peerless cone, the purple glory of its evening dress, its halo of sunset gold, you, too, will be bewitched and pray to be accounted among its happy children, saying, "Verily, Fuji San, like a great white presence, outshines every other light in the Land of the Rising Sun."

GILBERT AND RIVINGTON, LD. ST. JOHN'S HOUSE, CLERKENWELL ROAD, E.C.

www.ingramcontent.com/pod-product-compliance
Lightning Source LLC
Chambersburg PA
CBHW030915270326
41929CB00008B/706